This book has helped me immeasurably — namaste —

GENTLE CLOSINGS

*How to Say Goodbye to
Someone You Love*

Ted Menten

RUNNING PRESS
PHILADELPHIA, PENNSYLVANIA

Canadian representatives: General Publishing Co., Ltd.,
30 Lesmill Road, Don Mills, Ontario M3B 2T6.

International representatives: Worldwide Media Services, Inc.,
115 East Twenty-third Street, New York, New York 10010.

9 8 7 6 5 4 3 2 1
Digit on the right indicates the number of this printing.

Library of Congress Cataloging-in-Publication Data
Menten, Theodore.
    Gentle closings: how to say goodbye to someone you love / Ted Menten.
        p.   cm.
    Includes bibliographical references.
    ISBN 1-56138-004-0
    1. Bereavement—Psychological aspects.   2. Death—Psychological
    aspects.   3. Grief.   I. Title
BF575.G7M46 1991
155.9'37—dc20   91-52787
                                                                    CIP

Editor: Steven Zorn
Cover design by Toby Schmidt
Interior design by Nancy Loggins
Typography CG Palacio and CG Omega by Commcor
Communications Corporation, Philadelphia, Pennsylvania

This book may be ordered by mail from the publisher.
Please add $2.50 for postage and handling.
But try your bookstore first!
Running Press Book Publishers
125 South Twenty-second Street
Philadelphia, Pennsylvania 19103

CONTENTS

This book
is dedicated
to the memory of
Gregory Scott Cooper,
who tasted life and found
it bittersweet.

And to the memory of
Ed Sibbett, Jr.,
who in the
knowledge of death
found the meaning of life.

And to the memory of all
my little angels.

Thank you and Godspeed.

In 1981, two years before my first book about teddy bears was published, I was invited by members of a local teddy-bear lovers' club to join them at a hospital where they were giving teddy bears to critically ill children. I liked the people in this group and admired their benevolence. I had no idea then what the return on investment would be from their simple gesture. The gift of a small bear was reciprocated with the incredible gift of love.

By 1983, *The TeddyBear Lovers Catalog* had been published. By then, I was visiting hospitals and giving away bears on a regular basis. When I traveled out of town to promote my book, instead of sitting in my dreary, friendless, hotel room, I'd gather a bunch of bears and visit the nearest hospital, where I knew I'd make new friends.

As time passed I began to do more than give away bears; I also held drug-dependent babies who needed to be comforted. Several volunteers would take turns holding and rocking the babies. Later we did the same with the AIDS babies.

Perhaps the most heartbreaking words I ever heard were spoken by a nurse about the crack babies. When I asked if we were going to rock the endlessly screaming infants, she replied: "No, they cannot be comforted."

They cannot be comforted.

Those words, spoken with such certainty, burned in my heart like a hot poker. But if the crack-addicted babies could not be comforted, surely there were others who could, and I began to look for a way to be more useful.

Soon I found myself working with terminally ill children and adults.

To them I am the teddy-bear man, "Bear," or "Mister Silly." To me they are the teachers of joy and love. So close to death, they are the ultimate experts on the meaning of life, and on goodness, and honesty, and bravery.

In time I became a storyteller. Then I became involved in a process called closing, which is the way the living and the dying say "goodbye" and "I love you."

All of this just...happened. I am not a doctor. I am not a psychoanalyst. I have no degrees on my office wall. I haven't even got an office. I am simply a storyteller who goes where the stories need to be told, and where I can learn new stories. My training was all on the job.

The children, and later their parents, taught me everything I know. The nurses and the doctors shared their expertise with me as well. Everything I experienced made me re-examine everything I had ever thought and believed.

Since we are traveling together, I thought I'd share what I've learned with you. You don't have to believe what I believe, or question what I question, or even come to any of the same conclusions. We'll just walk together and talk things over.

I believe that there is a supreme being, a creator, because when I look around at the wonder and beauty of life, I can find no other reasonable explanation.

I like the idea of prayer. I think it is more sane to talk to someone else than it is to talk to yourself. (At first I had a problem with unanswered prayers until little Susan, age seven, explained it to me: "That's simple. God's answer was no.")

I like ghosts and reincarnation, too. A mystic once described my grandmother as an aura that followed me and protected me. That seems right enough; it's what she did before she died. I support recycling, so I suppose it is only natural to accept reincarnation. I might like to come back as something really special and magical like a butterfly or a teddy bear.

Heaven is a good idea, too. I like reunions; I like all that hugging and kissing and tears of joy when old friends get back together.

I believe that love gives the best return on investment.

I believe that truth is like a straight line—the shortest distance between two points.

I believe in second chances, and third chances, and fourth chances.

I believe that listening is essential to loving.

I believe in grief and sorrow and wailing and tears flowing like Niagara Falls. Tears mean something. They mean we're alive and feeling.

I believe that death is a friend, a fabulous dancer who will twirl me away in my last waltz.

I believe in taking the time to say goodbye and not putting it off until another day. Because more than anything,

I believe in love.

—Ted Menten
Spring, 1991

If you have ever stood in a busy railroad station and watched people leave one another, you may have noticed that no two couples say goodbye in exactly the same way—but each does it perfectly. Some hug and laugh. Some cling silently to one another with tears streaming down their cheeks. Some simply hold hands and gaze into one another's eyes, remembering the good times before this moment. And when it's time to leave, they take one long, last look, and then they let go.

This book is about letting go.

And if you have ever stood alone on a railroad platform, watching the last car disappear down the tracks, a wisp of steam trailing off into the sky, you will remember, too, the feeling of being left behind.

This book is about being left behind and feeling alone.

This book is about the process of closing—saying goodbye to the one you love who is dying. It's about people who have said goodbye, and how they found a way to do it.

This book will show you how you can find a way to say goodbye.

But this is not really a how-to book. This is more of a *how-you-might* book. In these pages, in these stories, you will not find easy answers or guidelines for success. But as you read each story, you'll find ideas, assurance, and, hopefully, the courage to say goodbye to the one you love who is going away.

If the one you love was forced to leave before you could say goodbye, there are stories for you, as well.

These are only moments, as fleeting as an eyeblink. Watch and listen, and take my hand.

We are standing in a hospital room in New York City. Looking out the window, I watch as the first rays of dawn turn the edges of the gray steel and glass skyscrapers to gold. A nurse is prepping her small patient for an operation he has only a ten percent chance of surviving. It's the only chance he has. I turn and smile as the nurse leaves, closing the door behind her.

"Bear?"

"I'm here, Sport," I reply.

"I'm afraid, Bear."

"What of?"

"Not the operation,"

"What, then?"

"Of not doing *it* right." He looks down, his large brown eyes filled with the fear that if death comes, he will not be ready.

"Don't worry, Sport, you'll be fine. You'll do it perfectly. Everyone does. It's the one thing we get right every time."

Terminal is one of those *nice* terms that doctors use instead of the real word. In this instance, the real word is death.

Art Linkletter collected the innocent, witty, and wise sayings of children. Here is one that I collected.

"I heard the doctor tell my mom that I was going to the terminal."

"Do you know what that means?" I asked.

"The terminal is where the trains leave from. I guess I'm going away."

People who know that they are going to die have an edge. All of us realize that sooner or later we are going to die, but we don't know when. Even in times of war, devastation, flood, or earthquake—even in the face of certain death—we are still uncertain. There are miracles. We count on them.

But sometimes death *is* certain, and when it is, the dying have the edge—the knowledge of *when*. That knowledge changes them.

Closing is a celebration of life and love. While those who have seen their timetable of life and death may choose to close more formally, there is no reason that those who do not have the edge should not do the same. In fact, we say goodbye to those we love every day—as kids leave for school, as we say goodbye to a friend who is leaving on vacation.

When we embrace and say "Goodbye, and remember that I love you," we are closing—not forever, but just for today.

If it should turn out that this was the last time we would be together, how much better we would feel had we embraced the one we love and said "I love you."

Coming to terms with death and accepting it as part of life is often easier for children than it is for adults. Perhaps, in their innocence, children simply accept the knowledge of death in the same way they accept all knowledge that is given to them—trustingly. Without the experience of living, a child does not comprehend what will be lost in death, and so is often better equipped to deal with the time left rather than looking at the time that will never be.

Adults, on the other hand, having seen life's map with its long and winding road, experience death as an interruption —an intrusion—of their lives. We speak so often of "life expectancy" that when we are faced with death we feel that it is unexpected instead of accepting that it is part of the natural process of life.

This first section deals with the knowledge of approaching death and how the process of closing begins. Many of the stories are about children and how, in their innocence, they come to terms with saying goodbye. Children don't have "life expectancy." They take life as it comes, one day at a time—one challenge at a time. Perhaps if we listen to them we will gain knowledge born of innocence, free of anger and disappointment.

What You Can Do

The answer to a question is often hidden within the question itself. When asked "What can you do?" I've found that the answer frequently can be found by rearranging the words into the answer: "Do what you can."

Not everyone is able to do the same things. Some people doctor, others nurse, and still others volunteer as candy stripers. Some raise funds, others contribute money. I tell stories and give away teddy bears in hospitals.

But there is one thing we all can do, and that is to listen. Everything I know is the result of aggressive listening. Most of us are passive listeners. Usually we're already thinking about our response, preparing our rebuttal. Our own thoughts and needs get in the way, and we don't even hear what is being said. When you are talking with someone who is approaching death or who lives day-to-day with the threat of death, you must listen with both ears wide open. And that isn't easy.

Only children speak directly. As adults our experiences have taught us to be careful—selecting our words cautiously so that we don't entrap ourselves. Often truth can only be heard by listening to what *isn't* said.

I find that if I sit directly across from someone and we hold hands, then purge my mind of anything personal, I can hear some amazing things. When I'm listening aggressively I never intrude or comment on what is being said. I prod a little to keep the flow going, or I respond with a nod or a facial expression that indicates that I understand or that I don't. I reassure the speaker by patting his hand or holding it more tightly.

Most of us are uncomfortable in the face of death. Usually we try to put on a happy face and act perky. But that's not being truthful, and if there's one thing that someone facing death doesn't need, it's a lie.

Children are especially good at sensing deception. It bewilders them because they usually fault themselves. If Mommy and Daddy are acting differently, the child feels he or she did something wrong. More than anything, kids fear rejection and abandonment. But then, don't we all?

By listening aggressively we learn what our loved one needs from us, wants from us. He will tell us when to draw closer and when to pull back, when to talk and when to listen. And when to face the inevitability that death is near.

Ideally, a closing is a shared experience. The person facing death may begin the closing. But if you sense that your loved one is resisting saying goodbye, you may choose to start the closing. How? Do what you can.

Talk of the life you have shared, recalling an amusing or special time. By doing this, you express the importance of this person and your relationship. Without saying it, you're indicating that you will miss him, that he will be remembered. No one wants to be forgotten.

Very often, when a disease is disfiguring, the loved one will withdraw—refusing to let anyone visit. Pick up the phone and call. Send cards. Write letters. When this happens I send clippings from magazines that I know will amuse or interest my friend. It says that I still think of him as part of the living world and that I remember what he enjoys about life.

And finally—and this is the most difficult part—I show my grief. Nothing is more grotesque than the masquerade of good cheer at the bedside of someone who is dying. That smiling face, or even the stiff upper lip, is no comfort.

Isn't it strange that standing on a train platform, saying goodbye to a loved one, we have no trouble with tears? Those tears are an affirmation of our love, our sorrow, and our pain of being separated. We rejoice in those tears—knowing that they mean we love and are loved in return. But somehow, when we face the final farewell of a loved one, we hold back those tears until after he is gone. Everyone is so busy being brave. Telling lies. Tears would be more truthful.

When someone you love is facing death, what can you do? Face it together and do what you can.

No Rules except One

Sitting in the hospital coffee shop, I'm stirring my coffee and wondering if I'll be able to handle working one-on-one with terminally ill children beyond just giving them a teddy bear to keep them company.

Across the table is my friend Big Mary. She's a nurse who has been working with terminal patients for many years. She's big-boned and solidly built, with small, delicate hands and long, fine fingers. Like me, she bites her nails. She always looks fresh and clean; she says it's not good for a nurse to appear messy, and she changes her uniform two or maybe three times a day. When she smiles she looks like a model for Aunt Jemima. When I tell her this, she says: "An' you look like a gray-haired Massa Lincoln, boy." She punches my arm and throws her head back, laughing.

When I tell her that I'm worried about doing this job, she grabs my arm and squeezes it firmly. "You'll be fine, just remember the rule."

"What rule?" I ask, bewildered. No one told me the rule.

"Ain't none!" she laughs again, tickled by the panic in my eyes. "Oops, yes, just one."

"What's that?" I ask, wondering if I can handle it.

"They get it their way."

"What?"

"The patients—the kids—they get it their way. All the time." She looks at me, suddenly serious.

"Look," she continues, "they know what's happening, and don't think for a minute they don't. Even the very little ones. So the best and kindest thing we can do is let them set the rules. They wanna talk—you listen up. They wanna be alone—you scoot. They wanna laugh, or cry, or swing from the trees—you let 'em."

"But. . ."

"No buts." She holds up a slim finger in warning: "You leave the driving to them. You just go along for company and to be there when they want you or need you. Trust me, they'll let you know what they want and need."

"I'm a little scared."

"Me too, every day for 11 years. It's good for you, keeps you sharp and alert. Let's go."

I pick up my bag of bears and follow her down the hall.

About 12 kids are sitting there waiting for me. Mary introduces me and tells them that I'll be helping her from time to time and that today I'll be telling them a story. And suddenly I'm on my own.

I don't know what I expected, but whatever it was, this isn't it. They sit there, watching me and waiting for me to do my thing. Later I'd learn that they were scared that I wouldn't like them, that I'd reject them because they were sick, because they were going to die. People come and go, and the children wonder if it's their fault.

I pull up a chair and face their unsmiling little faces. I feel like a bad vaudeville act playing to a hostile audience. I realize that my expression is just as apprehensive as theirs. What I need now is a taxi!

"Well, what kind of story would you like to hear?"

"Princesses."

"Baseball."

"Goonies from space!"

"OK," I reply, smiling, "a story about a goonie princess from outer space who plays baseball." No laugh. "Well, how about a goonie baseball from outer space who plays princess?" A giggle.

"Once upon a time there was a baseball who was so spaced out he wanted to be a princess..."

"That's dumb," shouts one kid.

"Yeah, that's dumb," chime the rest.

"Let's take a vote. Who thinks this will be a dumb story?"

It's unanimous. They all think it stinks.

"OK," I try again. "Once upon a time there was a land beyond time where everyone got one wish, but if they made the wish before it was the right moment, they didn't get it." Total silence.

"In this land lived a brother and sister who had run away from the evil King of Darkness. This is the story of how they searched for the good King of Light who was their real father." Total attention.

"The boy's name was Button and the girl's name was Blossom. As they traveled through the Kingdom of Darkness they met many friends and had many adventures, and today I'll tell you their first adventure: Button and Blossom and the Silver Reflection. . . ."

That was five years ago. Button and Blossom are still having adventures and they are still looking for the Kingdom of Light. They still have their one wish, which I have learned from the kids is:

"That Mommy and Daddy will always love me."

"That the King of Darkness will be destroyed."

"That my hair won't fall out."

"That I won't die."

It's their story, and I try to let them tell it their way.

Welcome to Harmony

Imagine this: You are standing in a
beautiful room filled with sunlight that streams through large,
open windows that reach from floor to ceiling. Outside, the air
is fresh and fragrant, the trees are bright green, and in the
distance you can hear songbirds. A gentle breeze blows
through the room, carrying the scent of spring grass and
budding blossoms.

In the center of the room two comfortable armchairs
face one another. Beside each chair is a table set with fine
crystal and china and an array of beverages and snacks.

Now imagine this: You are sitting in the chair that
you have chosen and you look up to discover that a man is
sitting opposite you. He has white hair and a white beard,
greenish-gray eyes and a ruddy complexion. He has a
gentle, whimsical smile. He is an older man, maybe sixty,
but in some ways he seems much younger. That
will be me.

Then imagine this: I am holding a very old, very worn,

very loved, honey-colored teddy bear in my lap. I smile and introduce myself.

"Hello, my name is Ted and this is my childhood companion, Bear. Some people call me Bear and him Ted. We answer to either name."

Now I extend my hand to you, and you extend yours and we shake.

"Welcome to Harmony," I say.

Harmony is the most beautiful place you can imagine. It is where everything that can't be worked out gets worked out. Harmony is a safe haven: a place where you can ask questions and get straight answers. It is where truth dwells.

Anyone who wants can come to Harmony. The very young and the very old are welcome. We gather in a circle and talk about life and we talk about death and about dying. And we talk about saying goodbye.

There are no rules in Harmony except that we must all try to be truthful. We must all try to listen. We must all try to be understanding of each other. We must try to try. If we mess up (and we do), then we hold hands and start over.

After nearly a decade of working within the limitations of existing hospital programs I began to feel the strain of bucking the system. As long as I delivered my bears, told my Button and Blossom stories and didn't get in anyone's way, I was welcome in almost any hospital across the country. But if I advised a family to take their loved one home to die, I was "out of line." If I suggested that a hospice might be a more loving environment than a hospital, I was "out of line." If I encouraged a patient to make a living will to prevent being hooked up to machines, I was "out of line." And if I suggested that patients have a right to die on their own terms, I was definitely "way out of line."

Nurses reported me for making too much noise (laughter), doctors complained that I gave advice, therapists thought that my methods were unconventional: who needed a teddy-bear man, anyway?

Of course, it wasn't all bad. In fact, it was mostly wonderful when I minded my own business and followed the rules. If I minded my Ps and Qs, everything went pretty smoothly and, for the most part, still does. I had no desire to undermine the system or go head-to-head with the administration. I just wanted to go on doing what I'd been doing, and maybe just a little bit more.

So I created the Harmony Project.

Now, in a pleasant, open space, away from the hospital, my friends and I can go to Harmony as often as we please without anyone telling us to quiet down when we laugh too hard. We can giggle or cry or roll on the floor or sit up all night talking if we want to. It isn't big and fancy, but it is Harmony.

In Harmony, I conduct quilting sessions for fathers who have lost children to AIDS, and workshops for widows who join together and mourn in a positive, honoring way. I work with terminally ill children and their families, separately and in groups.

I help raise funds for projects such as Ronald McDonald House and Meals On Wheels.

And I go on telling stories to children of all ages.

Today, many hospitals have bereavement counselors or grief counselors. These professionals do wonderful work helping families adjust to the loss of loved ones. But grief is only one aspect of death—only one part of the process of closing. It is the whole process of closing that concerns me.

If we are able to close, to say goodbye, and mean it in our hearts—if we can let go and be free to live and to love—if we can learn to honor and to accept the gift of remembrance, then we have completed our journey in Harmony and made a successful closing.

Who Is Death?

We are sitting in a circle holding hands and doing our breathing exercises.

We are seven and one, but we are not eight. Seven of us are terminal, and I am not.

"Is everyone in Harmony?" I ask softly.

"Yes," they reply.

"Does someone named Seth have a question?" I ask.

"What is it like to grow old?"

"How old?"

"Like you, Bear."

"Well, I'm not exactly that old. I'm 59, but I suppose that's old to you. I have backaches sometimes, and stiff joints, and receding gums. But inside I still feel like a kid. I may never really get to be old in my head. I may never grow up—like Peter Pan.

"Does someone named Samantha have a question?"

"How can I get my mother to stop being sad?"

"Anyone got the answer?" I ask. In Harmony, anyone can give an answer.

"Tell her it's OK that she's sad. Tell her that you'll miss her, too," says Bobby.

"Will I? Will I miss her after I die?"

"Anyone have an answer?" I ask.

No one speaks.

"I guess that one has to wait awhile. Does someone with the name Ivy have a question?"

"Who is death?" asks Ivy, who's seven.

"Death isn't a who," says Seth. "It's a what."

"Are you sure of that?" I ask.

"Come on, Bear, everyone knows that death isn't a person or a place. It's a thing." Seth is 12 and sure of almost everything. "It's just nothingness."

"I don't want to be nothingness," says Ivy, almost in tears. "I heard someone say that death took Jenny. So I know that it is a person and not a thing." She is determined.

"Ivy, if death were a person," I ask, "what do you think he'd be like?"

"Well, I'm not sure because everyone is always so sad when he comes, but then people always say that when you're dead you're at peace. So maybe he isn't really bad. Maybe he's a nice person with a bad job."

"You're crazy," blurts Bobby.

"Bobby, no one is crazy in Harmony. Harmony is where we can say anything. But now you've upset Ivy, so let's hold hands and breathe our way back to Harmony.

A few moments pass and I ask:

"Does someone named Bobby have a question?"

"After I die, will I come back as someone else?"

"Do you know what that is called?" I ask Bobby.

"Reincarnation. So will I?"

"Would you like to?"

"Sure, maybe next time I won't get sick and I can grow up and become a baseball player. And maybe next time I won't make my parents sad because I'm sick. They always try so hard not to look sad but I can always see it."

"Can you really choose what you come back as?"

"Is that your question, Susan?" I ask.

"Not really, Bear, but I would like to know."

"Well, nobody has ever come back and told us, but there are lots of people who believe that they have been other people before, and that they will be more people in the future. I like the idea of being a person again and again."

"Me too," says Bobby.

"Bear?"

"Yes, Ivy."

"I think I know who death is. He's the train conductor who takes us back and forth."

"Well, that's not such a bad job," I say.

"Yes it is," says Ivy earnestly. "It's a terrible job because he never gets off the train. He never gets to be alive."

Memorizing the Moment

The sun broke through the clouds and glistened like stars in the thousands of dewdrops that covered the green lawn in the early morning. The air was crisp and fresh, and the promise of a perfect day was expressed in the chirping of a dozen tiny birds as they shook their wings and danced in the dew-drenched grass.

I cut through the park, inhaling the clean air and feeling glad that it would be a day when I could take the kids outside to play.

I joined a few of the parents who were waiting on the hospital steps. Together we went to gather the kids for an outing.

As we walked down the hospital corridors I glanced at the faces around me. Tense and drawn, they all reflected the pain and worry that never left them. No one spoke in these few moments before we entered the children's room. Everyone was getting ready to smile, to act happy. On each face I could see the same struggle to find the smile.

Down the hall and around the corner, the children waited quietly. They, too, were in the process of finding the smile. They would give their parents brave little smiles of reassurance—little Jack-in-the-box smiles that would pop on their faces as the door opens and their families rush in and embrace them.

My job is to take care of the kids whose parents aren't visiting today and to organize an event that all the kids can do together. We decided to head over to the park and just fool around.

At the park we slipped into an easy round of Simon Says as we marched along.

"Simon says: hop, hop, hop like a bunny."

"Simon says: buzz like a bee."

"Simon says: growl like a bear."

"Hey, Bear, show us how you growl."

I hunch my back, screw up my face and do my best bear growl. It is intentionally terrible, sounding more like a sick cow than a fierce bear.

"That's awful!" they laugh. Then they show me some real growls, with bared teeth and slobbering tongues. Hands raised and fingers curled like claws, they chase me and grab my legs, growling and giggling until I surrender and admit that they are fabulous growlers. They run around laughing and growling at each other.

I look across at the parents. Each face has the same

expression. It is a wistful expression touched with pain and longing; a look that might at any moment turn into tears, but seldom does. And it is a look of intense focus, clear and unclouded—similar to the expression I'd seen on the faces of painters as they looked from model to canvas.

It is a look that etches every detail into the brain. Each parent is memorizing every detail of what is happening: the joy and the laughter, the sunlight in the trees, the sky above, the fresh scent of early summer, and their children standing with their backs hunched and their arms raised, growling like bears.

Simon says: memorize the moment.

Understanding

"Is everyone in Harmony?" I ask.

"Yes," they all reply.

"Does anyone have a question?"

This is not a group of terminally ill children, but the parents of the children. The kids love going to Harmony and have told their parents about the experience, so the parents have gathered tonight to join hands, do our deep-breathing exercises, and journey to Harmony.

"How can I tell my daughter that she is going to die? She's only six. How can she understand?"

"First of all, you don't have to tell her—the other kids will. They'll initiate her and then take her into their circle. A circle we are excluded from."

"Billy was just about her age when he went into the hospital," explains one of the parents. "After the first weekend he could pronounce all the names of the diseases and their treatments better than I could."

"But death—what can they understand about death?"

"The same as they understand life—in their own terms," I say. "Children ask hundreds—thousands—of questions, but if you listen to those questions, they're always in children's terms. Not the terms of the adult world. The mistake we make is that we don't answer them in their own terms.

"Once, a friend's daughter asked her where babies came from. The daughter was about four or five at the time. Well, my friend was ready with the answer and sat her daughter down and explained the entire process, starting with the glint in Daddy's eye right up to when they took Mommy's feet out of the stirrups. After she finished the story her daughter looked at her and frowned.

"'Not from cabbages?' she asked. Sometimes, the less you tell them, the better.

"But always tell the truth. Sick children have radar that tells them when you're lying."

Everyone laughs nervously because this is so true. Doctors, nurses, and parents all agree that kids have this radar. The truth is that it isn't radar at all. It's a keen sense of smell. The simple fact is that lying stinks and kids can smell it.

Believing

Much wiser, more profound, and more deeply religious minds than mine have pondered the meaning of life and death. Nevertheless, I'd like to share with you my perspective on death and afterlife.

Opinions about life, death, and beyond are, it seems to me, a bit like selecting seats on a commercial airliner. You can choose first-class seats, business-class seats, or economy. It really doesn't matter which class you pick because you'll get to your destination the same time as everyone else. Since we're all going to make that final journey, one way or another, the choice of class is simply a matter of comfort.

With this in mind I suggest the following procedure when you come to the terminal to say goodbye: Please respect the class that your loved one has chosen. Love is always respectful. Always. So keep that in mind when you hold the hand of someone you love when it's time to say goodbye. You may not share the same beliefs—God has a hundred names and a thousand faces—but no matter the name of the pilot, the destination remains the same.

I asked a group of children what they thought was going to happen when they died. Going to heaven was a popular destination.

"How will you get there?" I asked.

"An angel will come and get me," replied Wendy.

"Beamed up like on 'Star Trek,'" said Bobby.

"I want Lassie to take me," said little Sharon.

"But Lassie's only a dog!" said a disapproving Bobby.

"I know, but Lassie always knows how to get home."

Wishing

Being an only child has its highs and lows. You don't have to share your room, you never wear hand-me-downs, and you get all of your parents' love. But you're also the only one who can fill their expectations, and you always have to look for someone to join you on the seesaw.

When children become terminally or even critically ill, they might as well be only children because suddenly they are different from their brothers and sisters. And they ride a special seesaw called remission.

Remission is a second chance. A reprieve from a death sentence—but not a pardon. All patients welcome the news that they are in remission, but even the youngest are aware that they're on a seesaw with death on one end and life on the other. Their own lives are in the middle, sliding back and forth.

While it's difficult for the patients, it is harrowing for the family, who one moment are trying to come to terms with the idea that the child they love is dying, and then readjusting to the idea that he or she may live.

During this period of remission the process of closing is put on hold as the family rejoices. But everyone knows that if the therapy doesn't work, the closing process will have to begin again. Each time, saying goodbye becomes more difficult.

Susan is wearing a bright pink T-shirt bearing the message, LOOKING FOR A BLESSING. In Susan's case that means a remission.

"Hi, Bear, how's it going?"

"Tip-top—and you?"

"I'm working on my Wish Book."

"What have you added?"

"Well, I did Disney World last month, so that one's complete. And I just found out that my test scores were high enough for me to move on to junior high, so I can start thinking about that. And I got the computer I wanted, so now I'm looking around for another place to go on my next vacation."

For Susan, vacations come between remissions and treatments. She is a veteran of the seesaw, and so are her parents. Three years ago doctors gave Susan only a few months to live, and her parents began the process of closing. At least they took the first step—they accepted what the doctors told them and then started looking for a miracle.

"We decided to be receptive. To look and listen and wait." Susan's mother, Helen, holds her husband's hand. "Fred likes lists. So we started making wish lists. Remission was number one but we were practical about it."

"No unnecessary pain was number two," says Fred. "We didn't want our little girl to suffer. Then Susan started her book and we helped her. She set goals for herself and her disease. She began to visualize winning over her disease and pretty soon she got the first blessing."

"Now we plan the blessings and concentrate on them coming to us. It really works, you know." Helen smiles and pats her husband's hand. "We love and trust the Lord but we're not lazy. Fred says that if we want the Lord's blessing we have to help Him bring it to us. So that's what we visualize.

"We had to put death on the list, too. It wouldn't be realistic not to. Wouldn't be fair to the Lord not to accept that death might be a blessing. So we put it on the list."

"But we keep putting other things ahead of it," adds Fred. "Every time we get a blessing that gives Susan more time, we kind of move death down a notch or two. But we leave it there to remind us of all the good ones that came before it."

Susan's Wish Book and her parents' Wish List keep growing every day.

"Well, Susan, have you decided on your next wish?"

"Yes, Bear. I have and I got the idea from you."

"How's that?"

"I wished for white hair like yours. I wished to live to old age and have white hair. Of course I'll have to grow it back first."

Accepting

Most of the kids and a few of the grown-ups call me Bear or Ted. Some of the doctors call me Mr. Menten, just to keep things formal. But Jason calls me Mister Silly.

Teddy bears and laughter are my stock in trade. The bears are an expression of love and security and a first step toward trust. Laughter chases the shadows away. But more important is the fact that laughter reduces the span of years between us. When the kids and I laugh together we become the same age. It's magical.

When I first met Jason, he was a serious-minded young man of six. He had been in and out of hospitals since the day he was born. Now he was back again.

According to him, he wasn't afraid of anything anymore—he'd seen it all and was bored by the whole hospital routine. Jason wasn't interested in joining the rest of the children in games or listening to my stories. At the end of our first session he pronounced me *Silly*.

"You're silly!" he shouted at me. "You and your bear are silly." His face screwed up into an angry mask. "You're just a Mister Silly and your dumb ol' bear is silly, too."

He stuck his tongue out at me and turned his back. The other kids stood and watched, wondering what I'd do.

I leaned over and whispered into Jason's ear. "Mister Silly wants to be your friend. OK?"

But Jason wasn't that easily won. When you're six years old and have been sick day in and day out, it takes more than a silly man with a bag of bears to make you smile. He walked away and stood alone by the window, looking out, ignoring us all.

To children like Jason, grown-ups quickly become the enemy who poke and prod and feed you nasty-tasting liquids and give you enemas. They are the nurses and doctors who come and go with hardly a hello, frowning at your chart or your test results or your x-rays. And your parents always look so sad when they talk to the doctor.

I knew that I might never win Jason over, but if I did, it would be strictly on his terms. Right now he didn't want or need another adult in his life, especially one called Mister Silly.

Jason wasn't the only one who felt that way about Mister Silly. Doctor Gloomy didn't much like him either.

Of course Gloomy wasn't the doctor's real name, but it was what I called him. He worked with the AIDS patients, and no one ever saw him smile. The nurses and the interns warned me to keep out of his way. The families of patients, while admitting that he was an excellent physician, complained about his cool, almost brusque, manner.

Yet despite this, Doctor Gloomy's patients loved him. What appeared as clinical detachment translated to a directness that made even the worst prognosis bearable for his patients. His matter-of-fact attitude was coupled with incredible gentleness.

Late one Sunday, as I headed home after a long day in the children's ward, I saw Doctor Gloomy leaving a patient's room. As he pulled the door closed, he slumped against it. Then he turned to face the wall, holding onto it as though he would collapse without it.

I was sure that he hadn't seen me standing by the elevator. I was tempted to slip quietly away, but instead I walked over and leaned against the wall beside him. He didn't look up. I'm sure he assumed I was another staff member since it was long after visiting hours.

"I keep losing them," he muttered. "They just slip away and I can't help them. I'm supposed to be able to help them and I can't. I can't do anything. I just keep failing them."

"No, you don't," I said quietly.

He looked up at me, trying to place me. When he recognized me, he frowned.

"How could you understand? You're not a doctor."

"No, I'm not a doctor. And I won't presume to say that I understand what you're feeling. But I do know that part of your pain has to do with your refusal to let them go."

"What the hell is that supposed to mean?"

"It means that you're a doctor, not a god. You're a caregiver. Sometimes you save lives, because that's what you are meant to do—at that moment. But some day that life you just saved will come to an end and nothing you or any other doctor can do will stop that process."

"Don't lecture me," he snapped.

"Listen, you are a healer and a good one. Your patients love and trust you. Allow yourself that."

"But I keep losing them. One after another. They just...die."

"That isn't your fault. It isn't even your responsibility. Nobody is blaming you for their deaths."

"But they do blame me. Their families blame me. I'm supposed to help them. To heal them."

"You *are* helping. The families know you're doing all you can. It's just that they're so blinded by their grief, by their helplessness, that they cannot see that you are helping them. Because they are so powerless, they want you to be all-powerful. That simply isn't realistic. That's not your role. Patients do die. That is something between them and God."

"God?"

"Look, I don't know what you call it, but whatever it is

that terminates life is probably the same thing that created it in the first place. We have to accept it for what it is—the giver and the taker of life. And nobody, not even you, can change that. You are a caregiver, not a lifegiver. And if I'm presuming too much, I apologize. But in my own way I'm a caregiver, too, and my advice to you is to give them your best and then let them go."

"How would you feel if you'd spent years learning how to heal people and then suddenly everyone who comes to you for healing, dies?"

"I'd feel exactly as you do. I haven't any answers for that, Doctor, but I have a vision. In my vision, a red-eyed, exhausted research chemist is mixing components that will one day become the serum that cures AIDS."

I placed my hand on Doctor Gloomy's shoulder. "This is a war and you, my friend, are just a soldier. Whether we win this war depends less on you than on the munitions maker, that bleary-eyed chemist. But in my vision I know one thing for certain—as certain as I know my name is Mister Silly—that when that weapon is made and perfected, you and all the other doctors just like you will be on the front lines, using it to fight and win this war.

"Good night, Doctor."

"Good night, Mister Silly."

Rounds with Mister Silly

Gray days are the most difficult. Rain has a positive, refreshing aspect—like heavenly tears—but gray days simply cast gloom everywhere.

Believe me, there's nothing gloomier than a hospital on a cloudy day. So on gloomy days I must be especially bright and shiny, especially silly on morning rounds with my bag of bears.

The nurse from intensive care waves and signals that everyone is sleeping. I search for someone who is awake and has no visitors. I look into a room and spy an old friend who I haven't seen in a few weeks.

"Hi, Bear, wanna play doctor?" asks Kristen, a smiling 10-year-old.

"Sure. What's the disease of the day?"

"It's my kidney again." She purses her lips and frowns. "What do you prescribe?"

I do my terrible impression of Groucho Marx, but it gets a giggle: "Take two bears and call me in the morning."

I pull out two little bears and tuck them beside her.

"One will be enough, Doctor. I'm ailing but not failing."

"OK, but if you need a bear booster, I'll be just down the hall." I give her a kiss on the cheek and she gives me one back.

"Bear, don't tell Stanley that I kissed you. He gets jealous." Stanley is her real doctor.

I start down the hall and hear a giggle. I catch a glimpse of a little face peeking out at me from behind a door.

"I see you. We all see you! We're comin' to getcha! Here come the bears...!" I hear giggles and scurrying feet around the corner. I toss several bears into the room.

"Bear attack—everybody take cover!" I shout. Screams of delight. I wait a few moments before peeking into the room.

"Bear attack!" they scream in unison as the bears come flying back at me. I fall to the floor, clutching the bears and begging for help.

"Good morning, Bear," says my friend Mary, the nurse. "I see you're as well-behaved as ever. Children, pray to heaven that you don't grow up to be a silly man like this one."

"Mister Silly, Mister Silly, Mister Silly," they chant as they prance around me. I struggle to free myself from the bears and then get to my feet. The children hug my legs and beg for a story.

"Get your bears and grab your chairs. Mister Silly has come to town."

They rush around and fetch their bears. We pull the chairs into a circle. "It's Mister Silly Time."

An hour later I'm with the AIDS children, then the AIDS adults, and later the seniors. By five my bag of bears is empty. I'm tired and want a hot bath. Mister Silly has had a busy day.

As I head toward the front entrance, I pass an old fellow shuffling along the hall with his walker. He's wearing a plaid bathrobe, a grandpa gift robe I suspect—if he's lucky enough to have grandchildren. He stops and raises his hand to me in a silent greeting and then beckons to me. He wheezes when he speaks.

"You're that bear fella, ain't you?"

"Yes, sir, I am. My name's Ted. What's yours?"

"Henry. Henry W. Stone. W stands for Winthrop. Stupid name, Winthrop. My father didn't have sense enough to get out of the rain much less pick a name for a son. Should have listened to my mother. She had the brains. She was the one with the bright ideas. She wanted to name me Reynolds. Hell of a better name than Winthrop. Winthrop sounds constipated." He reaches for my arm.

"Listen," he whispers, "you give me a bear—a little one I can slip into my pocket—and I'll name him Reynolds. How's that?"

"OK, Henry, it's a deal. Next time I'll bring you a little bear for your pocket."

"No, tomorrow. You bring it tomorrow. You think I'm gonna live forever? This ain't my springtime, sonny, this is dead winter. Tomorrow. Early. I'm best in the morning before they stick something into anything they can pry open."

"OK, bright and early tomorrow, Mr. Stone."

I smile and pat his shoulder. He starts down the hall and then turns and holds up a finger.

"I know what they call you around here," he says. "Screw 'em. Don't you feel one bit silly." He smiles a crooked smile. "Early, remember."

"First thing." I wave goodbye and head home for that hot tub. Funny, the one thing I never feel is silly.

The Tiny Giant

Just being an adult puts great distance between me and the children I work with. Being 6'5", I'm well above the average height that kids are used to, and so it's even more important for me to attempt to get down to their size.

Often I tell them the story of Gulliver and the Lilliputians, or even how large Dorothy must have seemed to the Munchkins. If I let the children overpower me, it's even better. I've spent many an afternoon flat on my back with three or four kids sitting on top of me giggling with delight.

Since I use stories as parables to help kids deal with the various problems that befall them during their illnesses, it was natural for me to create a story about the most frightening giant of all—the adult.

• • •

Button and Blossom
and the Tiny Giant

As Button and Blossom approached the great forest at the edge of the Green Kingdom, they met an owl named Sidney.

Sidney had long ago stopped saying "Who, who, who" the way other owls did. Frankly, he no longer gave a hoot. He had read books and become wise beyond his years.

Sidney lived in a delightful house set in the elbow of a weeping willow tree at the edge of a pond. Button and Blossom were passing beneath the tree when Sidney noticed them and spoke.

"Good afternoon, children," he said, in his refined and educated voice.

Button and Blossom looked up and greeted him in return.

"What brings you two to the great forest?" asked Sidney.

"We are searching for the Kingdom of Light," replied Button.

"Do you know how to get there?" added Blossom.

"Well, you'll have to go through this forest, and that means dealing with the great, mean giant who lives at the very center and rules for a hundred yards in all directions. I hear that he has a terrible temper, and he's tremendously large and frightening."

"Oh, my," said Button.

"Oh, dear," said Blossom.

Button and Blossom set off through the forest. The forest got darker, and darker, and darker, but Button and Blossom held hands and weren't too afraid.

As they neared the center of the forest, they began to think about the giant who lived there.

"He must be very, very big," said Blossom, clutching Button's hand.

"Terribly, terribly huge," said Button, squeezing her hand in return.

They stood holding onto one another, imagining how horrible the giant might be.

"Do you think the giant will hurt us?" asked Blossom, trembling.

"I don't know," answered Button, "But Sidney seemed awfully afraid of him and he's older and wiser than we are."

They slowly walked toward the center of the forest. At the very center was a small clearing. In the center of the clearing was a tiny castle about the size of a dollhouse.

"Look at the little castle," exclaimed Blossom.

"I wonder who lives inside it?" wondered Button.

"I do, you big galoots!" said a tiny voice.

"Who are you?" asked Button.

"I'm the giant of the forest," replied the voice.

"I can't see you," said Blossom.

"Of course you can't, you ninny. You're too big!"

"But you're supposed to be a giant," remarked Button, bewildered.

"I *am* a giant! Sidney thinks I'm a giant. The field mice think I'm a giant. The bees and the butterflies all think I'm a giant. So I'm a giant!"

"But giants are supposed to be. . .well. . .*giant*," said Button.

"To some people I am gigantic and therefore a giant. It's relative, isn't it? And if you believe that I'm a huge giant, then I *am* a huge giant."

"But you're not," said Blossom.

"Not to you, you overgrown child. But to everyone smaller than me, I am. Now go away and stop bothering me, and, for goodness sake, don't step on my castle."

"We won't, little giant, we'll be very, very careful," said Button as he stepped over the castle and pulled Blossom after him.

"Big galoots," mumbled the tiny giant as he watched them trample through the tall grass.

· · ·

Getting problems down to size is important when working with children. We forget that the scale of our lives is much larger than the scale of theirs. If we want to help them we must get down to their size, or else we become galoots, trampling through the grass of their enchanted forest.

It doesn't take magic to make a giant tiny. It takes understanding of the reality of his true proportion in relationship to ours. So we, the parents, and doctors, and caregivers must endeavor to become tiny giants so that children will lose their fear of us.

The Bunny
and the Eggheads

One of my groups of kids is bald from either chemotherapy or radiation therapy. The children range in age from seven to 13. When they're alone they walk around without hats on—at least the boys do. The girls are embarrassed about losing their hair and tend to wear their hats.

Children adapt quickly and form tight circles from which outsiders are excluded. Although I'm an outsider who has all his hair, I'm not excluded from their games and their humor. In fact, I'm often the butt of their hairy jokes.

Among themselves the kids are called Eggheads. Of course I'm not supposed to know this because it's a secret and exclusive clan. Eggheads support and reassure one another as no outsider can. I consider it an honor even to be tolerated by them.

As Easter approached, the little girls were feeling some anxiety about wearing Easter hats. Bonnets were suggested but rejected as too babyish. None of them even considered wearing a wig. It was declared yucky.

As the time grew closer I decided on a plan that I thought they all would enjoy.

I checked around and found some water-base paint that could be used safely on skin, and then rented the most awful rabbit costume I could find. It was a terrible fluorescent pink and very, very tacky. The Saturday before Easter, I arrived at the hospital dressed in the bunny suit and made my way to where the kids were waiting for me. When I came in they got hysterical and it took quite a while to get them settled down. Then the fun began.

One by one I decorated their heads in bright colors like Easter eggs—flowers and butterflies and stars and dots and stripes. The more garish the better. At first only the boys let me paint them, but eventually the girls took off their hats and I painted their heads with ribbons and flowers and tiny hearts. We laughed as each head was painted until everyone had a colorful dome. Then I took off my bunny head and revealed my own bald pate. Of course it was a fake, but it could be painted and all the kids got to draw something on it.

Later, when the nurse came in, she nearly had a heart attack. The doctors didn't find it at all funny but the kids loved it. The next week they voted me an honorary egghead.

Laughter is a bridge.

Living with Dying

The trouble with truisms is that they are, generally speaking, true. Whether it's "live and learn," or "live and let live," or "love is blind," you can usually find evidence to support it.

So when I say that it has been my experience that those who have a knowledge of their approaching death generally react in one of two ways, you will understand I am speaking generally.

My truism is this: People who know they are going to die spend their remaining time either a) being alive; or b) staying alive.

The people who fit into the first category enjoy the time they have left. Those who concentrate on staying alive, however, spend every waking moment looking for a cure, running from doctor to doctor, drug to drug, hope to hope.

For people with AIDS, the desire to stay alive is urgent as they scramble for treatments to delay their deaths, knowing that a cure may be years away.

It's natural to want to survive. But often the frantic search for a wonder drug or a miracle cure only speeds the progress of the disease instead of retarding it. And all too often the process of staying alive destroys the process of being alive.

Again and again I have watched weeks of searching turn into months of searching, until the few remaining years dwindle away without any joy or happiness.

I knew and worked with Ed for 13 years. He was painfully shy. At parties he stood in the background; at dinners he almost never spoke. If someone remarked about how quiet Ed was, Ed would cheerfully reply, "Well, someone has to listen."

Ed was a wonderful artist. He was often invited to speak about his work to students, but he always politely declined. The idea of standing in front of even a few students and talking about himself filled him with terror.

Among our friends, I was called the mouth and he was called the ears. But the truth was that Ed had a lot to say in one-on-one situations. When we were alone, I was usually the ears. I once asked him why he never spoke up in a group; he replied that he never knew when it was his turn. I laughed, but to him it was a painful problem. Over the years I tried again and again to get him to try speaking to students, but nothing could get him to face an audience.

Then he contracted AIDS and nearly died of pneumonia. He left the hospital a changed man. Within weeks of his release he began publishing a newsletter titled *Healing Aids*, which described alternative healing techniques.

He and his partner, Doug, worked long hours researching and publishing the newsletter. Then Ed started leading discussion groups and workshops, sharing the information he had. No longer the shy man in the corner, he became a vocal and outspoken advocate of positive thinking. He gave up his career as an artist and spent every hour helping others to understand the transition we call death. He believed in and promoted all of the theories of self-healing coupled with traditional medical techniques.

"If crystals work for you," he'd say, "use them. But remember to take your AZT." He was a practical believer.

He worked as long as he could and then, as he became weaker, he encouraged Doug to carry on after he was gone.

It was Ed who taught me about closing, and he encouraged me to continue working with terminal patients even though he wished I'd spend more of my energy on "his side of the street," meaning his work with spiritual healing.

In all the years that I had known him, Ed had never been more alive than in those last years when he knew that he was dying. He used everything he knew to stay alive and then he devoted himself to being alive.

Tears to Shed

William Shakespeare wrote, "If you have tears, prepare to shed them now."

Not everyone has tears, and Shakespeare realized that when he began his invitation to sorrow with the word "if."

Now, I'm a real crier. The trouble is, I usually cry only when I'm happy. When Lassie comes home after being lost, I cry. I grew up in the golden age of movies when good things happened to good guys like Jimmy Stewart. I start to sniffle at the opening credits of *It's a Wonderful Life*.

You'd think that someone who sheds a tear at the drop of a rainbow would be a real mess doing the work I do. The truth is, I never cry when I'm working. I might cry later, and I've cried while writing this book, because remembering all those wonderful friends makes me as happy as when I first knew them. Now that they're gone, when I think about them, I cry. Because I can't pick up the phone and call them.

But they live in my heart and in their letters and pictures and a thousand mementos. I have videos and tapes and postcards from everywhere. Sometimes I'll go back to a special place we shared and celebrate our friendship by enjoying the day. Or I'll play my records.

I have this incredible patchwork quilt of a record collection. My knowledge of music is based on my friends and the music they introduced me to: classical, country and western, electronic, and punk rock. I love Madonna because that was Lucy's music. Eight years old and rapidly approaching thirty, Lucy could lip-sync every one of Madonna's songs, and she had all the moves.

Movies and their theme music take me a thousand places. And chocolate—the smell of chocolate—belongs to Greg.

Grieving is a natural part of closing. Sadness, loneliness, longing, and tears are the hallmarks of grief. In time, if we allow ourselves to, we leave grief and move on to honoring and remembrance. Then we step back through the portal into life, successfully completing the process of closing.

Tears are not the exclusive property of grief. Even after a successful closing, tears may still be shed. But these are not necessarily tears of grief.

I often wonder where tears of grief end and tears of joy begin. Sometimes I wonder if we really understand why we are crying. Or if we even need to know. To me, tears are just another blessing—like sudden summer rain—warm, unexpected, and fun to splash around in.

There are many ways to say goodbye, and all of them are good. Maybe even like death, they are perfect.

Several charities such as the Starlight Foundation and the Make-A-Wish Foundation grant wishes to children with life-threatening diseases. These very ill children, some of whom may be terminal, and their families are the guests of the host charity who is granting the wish. One of the most popular wishes is a trip to Disney World. This fun-filled vacation may be the last experience that the family has together away from the hospital; it gives the child and the family a happy image to remember during the difficult time ahead. After the child is gone, it remains a cherished memory.

While this is not a formal closing, it can be a step in the closing process. When my best friend was dying and while he could still get around, we took a vacation and looked back on the years of our friendship. Today, that's one of my strongest memories of him, rather than the darker days of his passing.

The first time I witnessed a closing, and long before I

heard it called that, was in the movie *Harold and Maude*. The film is about a vital old woman, Maude, played by Ruth Gordon, who has a love affair with a morose young boy, Harold, played by Bud Cort. They both enjoy funerals, and that is where they meet.

In one of the most touching scenes, the two sit on the shore of a lake. Harold gives Maude a coin from a carnival machine with "Harold loves Maude" engraved on it. Maude holds the coin for a moment against her heart and then tosses it into the water. Harold is bewildered by her gesture, but then Maude turns to him and says: "So I'll always know where it is."

The film is about how Maude gives Harold the spirit and joy of life while she gets ready for her death. And when she dies, they both are ready, even though Harold wants her to go on living. In the final scene we witness Maude's triumph as Harold embraces life on his own.

Saying goodbye can be a joy.

As death approaches we do not need to turn away in fear. Instead we can choose to celebrate life and join hands with those we love. We can sing and dance and make merry in the face of the lengthening shadow. We can take the time that remains to add a few magical moments to our book of memories. And when twilight falls and the moon rises and the one we love passes from us, we can take solace in the knowledge that we embraced and said goodbye.

Dave's Garden

When it was clear that Dave was going to die, he and Joan began a beautiful closing. They loved one another very much and had not had much time together before Dave became sick. To all of us who knew them, their love seemed like a miracle because they had both been looking for a partner for a long time.

They were strong for each other and spent their remaining time being as happy as they could. And that happiness was shared with everyone they knew. Separately they had always been generous people, always concerned about the welfare of those they cared for. Together they brightened everyone's life. The idea that Dave was going to leave us was too terrible to consider. The closing they planned for us was one of the kindest and most gentle that I know.

We each received a letter inviting us to a garden party for Dave. We were to bring a plant that would be placed in Dave's garden among all his favorite plants—his plants and ours growing side by side in a friendly memory.

Now, after Dave is gone, Joan can sit in his garden and remember the sunny day when friends joined together to say goodbye. She can tend Dave's garden as she tended him, with love and devotion. Together they planted a living, growing memory, bright and beautiful and sweet with the fragrance of life.

You Light Up My Life

Rusty loved the ocean. He loved the smell and the sound of the surf as it crashed against the beach. When he was very little he would run back and forth chasing the waves. His parents took home movies of him as his little legs carried him across the sand. He wobbled like a sandpiper and made tiny, birdlike footprints in the sand. And he thought that seashells were magical. To him they were wishes granted by the king of the sea. If you listened closely, the seashells told the stories of the wishes.

Rusty filled boxes and boxes with his shells and he listened to their stories of wishes granted. Ten years old and stricken with AIDS, he wondered if he could find a magic shell that would grant his wish for life.

We sat together and he showed me his shell collection. His cousins and friends at school had sent him shells. Some were from as far away as Hawaii and South America.

In the last weeks of his life, Rusty looked for a way to

leave something of himself for his parents, something they would remember him by. And he wanted to use the shells. I told him about a gift that my friend Ed had made for me. We agreed that it was perfect. Rusty selected the shells and I picked up the rest of the parts.

A week before he died, Rusty completed his gift to his parents. He had made a beautiful lamp. The base was clear glass and filled with shells. More shells were glued to the parchment shade. Each shell had been carefully selected for its beauty and its hidden story. When the lamp was lighted, the shells glowed from within.

On a beach somewhere a child, running toward the waves, stops to pick up a glistening shell. She puts it to her ear and listens to its song—Rusty's song.

The Voice of Silence

Today, in hospitals across the country, volunteer programs include everything from teaching crafts to telling stories. One of the first things I did when I began working in hospitals was to rock babies.

There are many reasons why babies need to be rocked and why hospitals need volunteers to hold babies in their arms and rock them. Nurses are now so overworked that they haven't the time. The increasing numbers of AIDS babies, drug-dependent babies, and abandoned babies makes the job of nursery caretaking monumental. So volunteers are needed to rock the babies.

One early evening I sat in a rocker with a baby in my arms. I was cooing to her in my usual manner when a nurse said to me, "She's deaf, Ted. She can't hear you."

I smiled at the nurse and answered, "I know, but she can feel me."

From time to time I am called upon to sit vigil with a

patient who is dying. Again, the shortage of staff or the absence of family makes it necessary for volunteers to perform this task. If a patient is not being monitored by a machine, then he or she needs someone to keep vigil. It is usually silent work. It is listening work. It is the eloquent voice of silence— unheard but felt.

Very old people who have slipped into their secret world beyond our reach, people in coma, patients with burning fever, and those who have, for one reason or another, shut out the world all respond to the voice of silence. As a storyteller I began to wonder if this silent voice might have a vocabulary of its own, much the way signing is the voice of the deaf.

And I found that it did. At first, mere touching was a kind of voice. Hugging, stroking, rubbing, and the range of tactile expression between these "words" were felt and responded to. In time some patients knew me by my touch and often acknowledged me by a gesture. Often they held me as I held them, and together we conversed in silence.

People are living longer than ever before and they are becoming more difficult to care for. Years ago our grandparents lived and died at home. Today we have institutions that house old people who need to be looked after, who have nowhere else to go, nowhere else to die. If they are fortunate, they will be comfortable, well cared for, and can expect their families to visit from time to time. And when they die, a loved one will be at their side.

Saying goodbye to a parent or grandparent is most difficult in the impersonal setting of a hospital or nursing home. While extending life, modern medicine has also extended the process of dying so that today people do not so much die, as drift slowly away. If we are not alert, our loved one may slip far from us and we may not be able to close.

Reaching someone who has slipped away is like gazing into a pond. Just as a still pond reveals more than a rippling one, only through stillness can we connect with our loved one. We must be careful not to stir the waters. When our loved ones can no longer hear our words, we can reach them with the voice of silence.

We must share the stillness, the serenity, and let ourselves feel the closing. We can look into the unseeing eyes and see ourselves reflected. We can rejoice that we are still together, even in silence. And we can hold one another and gently rock together, fluent in our silent language.

"To Whom It May Concern"

The need to say goodbye is a two-way street, but sometimes it is traveled alone in one direction. When death comes suddenly, unexpectedly, the person left behind must find a way to say goodbye and to go on living.

But what about the person who is dying alone? Across the country, our cities are crowded with the homeless, the derelict, the unemployed, and the generally unwanted. In solitude they wander from place to place, leaving no trail. No one knows their names, or cares to. Only death can find them.

Then there are the other solitary souls, who are just as alone when death calls. They live in tiny apartments with 12 locks to keep out reality. They are housed in nursing homes, and retirement villages, and a hundred other kinds of caretaking facilities. There they sit, waiting for that last caller to come and whisk them away. Many, their bodies racked with endless pain, don't wait for death's invitation and decide to put an end to their own misery.

Susan, a volunteer visiting nurse, tells the story of one

fragile, elderly woman who sat day in and day out in her one-room apartment. One morning Susan found her dead from swallowing rat poison. Pinned to her sweater was a note: "To whom it may concern: Goodbye."

As people live longer, they often outlive their friends and family. They find themselves without anyone to hear their goodbye. They have no closing with life. But a growing number of people are responding to this need to answer the call for one "whom it may concern."

Volunteers visit isolated AIDS patients, the elderly in nursing homes, and the mentally impaired. They come and listen, bringing teddy bears, pets, food, and love. They encourage people to begin the process of closing by sharing their memories of who they were and how they came to be who they are now.

A few days after Susan found her patient dead, she discussed her feelings with me.

"At first I felt terribly guilty. I felt that I hadn't done enough for her. But now I know that there really wasn't anything else I could have done. She was very old, very tired, and very much alone. We did talk from time to time, but she never even asked me my name. She called me simply 'nurse.' That was her way of keeping me at a distance.

"Maybe she was afraid to get close to me because that

might be too difficult, too painful. So now I think I see that what I did was right, and I understand that what she did was right—for her.

"I have accepted her note personally even though it was written impersonally, like a business letter. I was—I am—the 'whom' it concerned, who was concerned. I accept her goodbye and I'll honor her and cherish her gift of remembrance.

"I'm sure that she has closed and found her peace, and now so can I."

The White Space

Only a few decades ago, people died at home surrounded by their loved ones. Often, in their final moments they saw God, or angels, or some other unworldly guide who came to take them in death. This experience often comforted those who remained behind.

Now, because of technology, we are able to intervene and retrieve someone who is technically dead. In many cases these people report experiences that involve visitations by guides who taken them to a clear, white, peaceful space.

It is not important whether these reports are true; their value is that these near-death experiences provide comfort to the dying and to their survivors.

The classic near-death journey is populated with guides, often familiar, who beckon the dying person forward or lead him back to life. Some people report being told "this is not your time, you must return." Others, tempted by the beauty of the white space, must be forced back, being told that they have a purpose in life that must be completed.

One of the reported effects of near-death experiences is that the people who have returned no longer fear death. They also seem to have gained an enlightened sense of life and its worth. Often they emerge with a new sense of purpose and a direction to their lives.

Patients in the last stages of life often need to be monitored. A vigil is set up so that they are never alone. During the last moments of life, some patients speak of seeing God and the angels. Their eyes open and they seem to brighten and become alert, and then they are gone. The entire experience amounts to a matter of seconds, but it leaves a lasting impression on the person keeping vigil. One nurse commented to me that she could not decide if she felt the presence of death or the presence of God. I wonder if there is any difference.

In Harmony

I'm sitting in a circle with a bunch of kids who have cancer and are listed as terminal. They have all been through the same routine: the tests, the treatments, the baldness, and the remissions. They make nervous jokes about the frozen smiles and long faces on their parents, the nurses, and the doctors. They wish the grownups would really, truly smile and stop pretending.

The children range in age from seven to 11, but here in Harmony they are all one age. The age before death.

We're in the closing moments of our time in Harmony and I have discovered that this is usually when one of them will ask an impossible question, such as "What is the meaning of life?" or "Who is God?" The easy questions, like "Why am I going to die?" they can answer themselves.

"Well, it's almost time to leave Harmony," I say, smiling. "Does anyone have a last question?"

"When's lunch?" asks Jack, our newest member and clearly a bright young man with his priorities in place.

The very young and the very old seem to deal with death more directly than people in the middle years. Old folks, having lived a full life, no longer fear death. Children, in their innocence, seldom see beyond tomorrow, and so they don't think of death as depriving them of a future.

An important aspect of my work is to prepare everyone involved in the closing experience. Young children usually don't comprehend death. It is important not to frighten them. In computer parlance, I must make death "user-friendly."

In the form of a fable, the Button and Blossom stories address every aspect of approaching death, but some of the very young children don't understand the symbolism. So I have smaller stories that are more like familiar bedtime stories.

One of the kids' favorite stories (and my favorite, too) is based on a familiar Sunday school tale our pastor loved to tell about a little boy who had to go to church with the grown-ups. Later, when the boy's friends asked him what the grown-up services were like, he replied that they were boring, except for one thing: they sang a song about a cross-eyed bear named Gladly. Of course the boy was referring to the traditional hymn, *Gladly, the Cross I'd Bear*. A child's mind is a wonderful thing.

I've always loved that tale, so I created this story about a little bear who had a big job.

· · ·

Gladly, the Cross-Eyed Bear

The Angel of Death was given a vacation and told to

find a helper who would do his job while he was away. The Angel of Death asked the other angels if they would take his place, but they all were too busy. The Angel of Light said no, the Angel of Darkness said no, the Angel of Rainbows said no, and even the Angel of Odds and Ends said no, although he had nothing specific to do.

Finally the Angel of Death went down to earth to see if he could find a helper. Everyone turned away and refused even to talk to him. So he wandered from place to place until he came to the city dump, the place where unwanted things were discarded. The Angel of Death felt unwanted, too, so he thought he might find someone there who would be willing to help him out.

Sitting high atop a pile of trash was a tattered old teddy bear with crossed eyes and a silly expression.

"Hello," said the Angel of Death. "My name is Death and I'm looking for a helper. Are you available?"

"Hello, Death," greeted the bear, his smile getting wider. "My name is Gladly, and I seem to have nothing to do but sit here on this pile of trash and feel unwanted."

"Well," said Death, "being unwanted is perfect experience for this job."

So they struck a deal and Death left for his vacation. He gave Gladly a list of the people he had to fetch, and Gladly looked forward to completing his first assignment.

He found the house where Bobby lived with his

parents and a small brown dog named Woof.

Gladly climbed the stairs to Bobby's bedroom and crept quietly onto Bobby's bed. He was so quiet that even Woof didn't hear him.

Gladly sat on the bed and waited. Soon Bobby woke up. He rubbed his eyes and looked at the raggedy teddy bear sitting on his bed.

"Hello," said Gladly in as charming a manner as possible. "My name is Gladly, and I am temporarily the Angel of Death. I've come to take you to heaven. Let's go."

"Hello, Gladly," replied Bobby politely, trying not to snicker at the silly looking bear who seemed so determined. "I'm not ready to go with you yet. Let's hang around here a little bit longer. Do you like to skateboard?"

"No," said Gladly. "We're on a tight schedule and the Angel of Death told me that there were no ifs, ands, or buts about it."

So Gladly took hold of Bobby with his soft paw and they caught the cloud express.

"Gladly," asked Bobby, "will you go back and get my parents and bring them to heaven, too?"

"Yes, some day," replied Gladly with a sweet smile. He stuck out his chest, feeling proud of his new job and his first successful assignment. "That's my job!"

•   •   •

Acceptance of death is never easy. Perhaps if we could put our fear behind us and illuminate the passageway ahead we would have an easier time. Still, those are not easy tasks.

But once we have worked our way through anger, and denial, and avoidance, and bargaining, and promising, we come at last to that more peaceful space called acceptance. From that place we can more easily find our way to peacefulness.

Stories not only teach and explain, but reassure us as well. Death is certainly less frightening in the form of a raggedy teddy bear. Perhaps if we adults join the children sitting cross-legged on the floor with their milk and cookies and listen to the stories with their ears, death will seem less frightening to us as well.

Laugh and Let Go

It's no secret that laughter can be a healer. In *Anatomy of an Illness as Perceived by the Patient*, Norman Cousins describes how he healed his cancer with laughter, and there are hundreds of other examples of people who chuckled their way to health.

Since closing is essentially a healing process, laughter can help. Sometimes, when emotions are raw and despair is deep, a good laugh is the only medicine. It puts things back in perspective. After the crying has stopped, acceptance—and laughter—can begin.

Aunt Lucy had an iron will, a sharp tongue, and a reputation as a penny-pincher. Nothing was ever wasted. Wrapping paper was smoothed out and neatly refolded. String was wound onto an ever-enlarging ball. Aluminum foil had an afterlife that would turn Shirley MacLaine green with envy.

Lucy's niece, Barbara, lived with and cared for Aunt Lucy after her own mother's death. While there was a loving bond between them, it was often expressed sharply, through biting humor. Each had a long list of things they found intolerable about the other.

"You're cheap!" accused Barbara.

"You're a spendthrift!" snapped Aunt Lucy.

Their good-natured bickering went on and on, adding spice to their afternoon tea.

In her declining years, Aunt Lucy began to plan for that great day when she would (as she put it) "meet her Maker." Most of the planning concerned what she would wear to her funeral. As time passed, she became almost fixated on her choice of lingerie. She had always been a staunch and vocal advocate of clean undergarments. All the usual reasons were given, including windy streets and, most popular, being struck down by a bus and rushed to the hospital where—heaven forbid!—doctors and nurses would be forced to stop all lifesaving measures in the presence of less than perfect panties.

Week after week Aunt Lucy traveled to the shopping mall where she purchased lacy unmentionables in which to meet her Maker. At first this seemed harmless enough, but it wasn't long before this diversion took the proportions of an outright obsession.

Underwear fueled the fire between Barbara and Aunt Lucy. They argued about it night and day. Aunt Lucy was fiercely determined to meet God Almighty in the best undies money could buy; Barbara, nerves frayed and patience dwindling, was just as determined to have Aunt Lucy carted away to the loony bin.

I took tea with them one afternoon and tried to smooth the waters. Barbara was close to her breaking point as we walked together in the garden.

"Barbara," I said gently, "Lucy's a wonderful old lady who's scared of dying. All she dares to focus on is how she will look when she has to stand before the pearly gates and explain why all her life she pinched pennies until they howled. Give her a break and try to smile about it. You don't really care about the money she's spending, do you?"

"Of course I don't," said Barbara, smiling. "It's just so silly and she won't see it. For years she's played the eccentric, but she knew it and had a twinkle in her eye about it. But this—this is too serious."

"Death *is* serious, especially if you're terrified of it. And I think Aunt Lucy is terrified, despite the bluff."

"What can I do?" sighed Barbara, exasperated.

"Join the fun." I put my arm around her shoulder and she leaned her head against it and heaved a sigh.

"I'll try," she promised.

During the next few weeks Barbara helped Aunt Lucy with her shopping. They laughed together as the dresser drawers filled to bursting with lingerie. Finally they narrowed the selection to seven pair, which they put into a beautiful, scented box, to await that special day. It came sooner than either of them expected. Perhaps, having made her selection, Aunt Lucy felt comfortable about going to meet her Maker.

I attended the wake. Aunt Lucy looked beautiful in her gray wool Chanel suit. Her mother's pearls cascaded down her bosom until they reached her white-gloved hands, which held her worn Bible. She was every inch the perfect lady.

"You don't think she looks. . .er. . .stout?" asked Barbara.

"Stout? No, why?" I wondered what she was getting at.

"Good. I was afraid she might. She hadn't made her final lingerie selection before she died. We'd narrowed it down to seven ensembles but. . ." she lowered her voice, "You know how fussy she was. I decided to let her make the final choice."

"Are you saying what I think you're saying?" My mind reeled.

"I had her dressed in all seven of them. She can choose when she gets there." Barbara looked up at me and winked.

God and What's-His-Name

Growing up Protestant in the suburbs of New York during the early days of World War II, I was dutifully sent off to Sunday school while my parents caught an extra forty winks before getting ready for church.

My grandmother, who lived with us, was a bit of a character. My childhood was filled with stories of her youthful escapades, which made Hans Christian Andersen seem dull. In my memories, my grandmother seems more than a bit magical.

She had opinions on almost everything, whether she was interested in the subject or not. She was not in the least interested in religion, but God was a different matter. My grandmother and God were on good terms.

Twice a year she went to church: Easter, because she had a new hat, and Christmas, because she like to sing carols.

When I was 14, my grandmother learned that she had cancer. In those days there were few treatments and almost no chance of survival. During the next two years I watched the cancer slowly diminish her until she was as fragile as a glass figurine.

She never complained about the pain, only the inconvenience of being stuck in bed. She had always been active—a born dancer, as she described herself. And she was. She always seemed surrounded by her own music as her fingers danced through her knitting or pie baking.

"I was very jolly when I was a young girl." She'd look at me and wink. "Marry a jolly girl and you won't be sorry."

Toward the end she had trouble being jolly, but she never seemed depressed. We'd sit and talk about what was happening in my life. We talked about her dreams and adventures and all the things we loved to do together, especially the things my parents didn't approve of, like eating at the local deli instead of having "a good hot meal."

I knew she was slipping away when she told me that she'd seen God and What's-His-Name outside her window giving her the eye. I asked her who "What's-His-Name" was and she smiled and winked.

"The jerk you get the last dance with. The one who's always hanging around waiting until all the good times have passed and all that's left is the last waltz. Then he comes up and taps you on the shoulder and says this one is his. As much as you don't want to go, you know you can't refuse. So off you go. He's probably not a bad dancer. He's had a lot of practice."

One afternoon about three days before Grandmother accepted the last dance, the minister came in and sat with us. Grandmother graciously received him, despite the fact that she found him unamusing: her most deadly criticism. She was in one of her whimsical moods and teased him about his seriousness.

"God's work is serious business, Laura." he confided.

"Didn't God create laughter?" she asked with a sly smile.

"Yes, I suppose he did."

"Well, Pastor, I suggest you avail yourself of some."

"Thank you, Laura, I'll try to remember that. Are you ready to meet God?"

"Is He ready for me seems more to the question," she replied, laughing. "I'm always ready for what's wonderful... wonder is my favorite thing."

He left shortly after that and I watched her lying there, smiling to herself.

"Gran, what about God? Do you think you'll get into heaven?"

"I learned a long time ago—never want to go to a party that you haven't been invited to."

"But, we're all supposed to want to go to heaven."

"You know as well as I do, darling, that wanting isn't getting." She patted my hand. "But I'll tell you this, if the invitation comes, I'll be pleased to accept."

A Hug

When AIDS first cast its deadly shadow across America, the nightmare was so new, so terrifying, that everyone drew back in shock and fear and ignorance. Strong, young men entered the hospital and within weeks died, ravaged by an onslaught of strange diseases that reduced them to helpless, frail shadows of their former selves. The result was a plague mentality, and the response was to isolate—actually to alienate—the patient.

Fear is not our best or most honorable face, but in those first days fear was the only face that people with AIDS ever saw. Patients were confined to isolation wards where everyone who entered the room was masked, gowned, and gloved. Doctors wouldn't treat, nurses wouldn't tend, and morticians wouldn't bury.

Today the fear is slowly beginning to subside. Ignorance is giving way to enlightenment, and people are starting to act like human beings again. But in those darkest days, my life was changed.

Mary, one of the more humane and courageous nurses, grabbed me as I strolled down the hospital corridor on my way to the children's wing. She asked if I knew what AIDS was. I said yes, I did. She wanted me to take a teddy bear to a young man—one of *them*.

The teddy bears I give away are named Hug. They are based on a comic-strip character that I created. That afternoon, after receiving my mask, gown, and gloves, Mary took me into her patient's room. I think I was trembling; I know I was apprehensive. Mary explained to Billy that I wasn't a doctor, just a funny guy who gave away teddy bears. And then she left us alone.

Billy and I looked at each other for a moment, and then I reached into my knapsack and pulled out one of my bears.

"Would you like a Hug?" I asked cheerfully as I extended the bear to him.

"Sure," Billy replied with a strained smile.

I placed the bear in his arms. He stroked the soft fur and nuzzled the face.

After a while we talked. It seemed pretty normal considering I was sitting across the room, wearing so much protective covering that only my eyes showed, and all I could see of him was what little the disease had left. It might have been easier in the dark or if we had both been blind.

I didn't know it then, but we were having a closing. We talked about everything he wanted to talk about. We never mentioned death. That was an unspoken agreement. When the time came for me to leave he asked, "Would you give me a hug?"

I misunderstood his question and replied, "That Hug is yours to keep."

"No, Ted, not the teddy bear...a real hug."

I turned to Mary who was standing by the door, waiting for me. She nodded yes and then shrugged, which I took to mean that it was up to me.

"OK, what kind of hug would you like," I quipped, "father, brother, friend, or lover?"

"Friend."

We hugged.

The next time I saw Mary she handed me an envelope from Billy. He had died. Inside the envelope was a snapshot of a bright, smiling young man—full of life. On the back he had written: "To my hugging friend from Billy—in better days."

I Am Father, I Am Son

Perhaps of all the aspects of the death process, the most difficult to understand and deal with is rage. Rage afflicts the one who is dying and those who are left behind. Even when we find a way to deal with the fear and the denial and the refusal and the bargaining, we can still be destroyed by the rage.

Dylan Thomas wrote, "Do not go gentle into that good night...Rage, rage against the dying of the light." While anger and rage are natural parts of the dying process, each person expresses them differently.

As more and more people succumb to AIDS, we see many kinds of anger and rage. AIDS is always fatal and everyone knows it. Many of those who have contracted AIDS are young homosexual men. Often they are caught in a double bind. They must first tell their families that they are gay, and then that they are dying.

Their parents also face a dilemma. Sons suddenly become strangers. Parents feel betrayed. Love turns to rage. In some families, a child's death is easier to accept than his homosexuality. Sometimes, by hating the homosexual, the parent can rationalize that his death is for the best. But this rationalization is a denial that prevents the closing process.

I would like nothing better than to be able to offer some comforting words to parents and children caught in these circumstances. However, I think a greater lesson can be learned from the story that follows.

James had survived AIDS for almost three years, but now he was tired of fighting. He wanted to let go. He wanted the peace that came with death.

His mother, Sally, and his lover, Stan, sat beside his bed, each holding a fragile hand. James, once a robust young man, was now merely a fragment.

The late afternoon sun filtered through the slanted blinds of his hospital window and cast a pattern across the wall. James watched the pattern shift and lower as the sun eased toward the horizon.

"Where is he?" James asked.

"Your father's downstairs," replied his mother, looking to Stan for some help that he couldn't give.

"Isn't he coming up?" asked James.

"I don't think so, honey," she replied gently. Her hand stroked her son's thin fingers.

"That bastard!" said James, his voice filled with rage.

He started to cough. His mother took her handkerchief and wiped the saliva from the edge of his lips.

"Don't get yourself upset, honey. You know how he is."

"Yeah, I know. He's sitting down there waiting for his embarrassing faggot son to die so he can forget the whole thing and pretend I never existed."

"James, it isn't like that," his mother insisted.

"Like hell it isn't."

Stan reached up and ran his fingers gently through James's hair. They looked at one another and smiled. Their smile.

"Easy, man, just take it easy." Stan's voice was soft and touched with the melodic tones of the Deep South. "You know these good ol' boys take a bit of coaxing. He'll come around. Just give him a little time."

"I don't have much time," replied James, closing his eyes.

Downstairs, James's father sat chain-smoking and grinding his teeth. From time to time he'd flip through the magazines without really looking at them and then get another unwanted cup of coffee. His rough, calloused hands clenched and unclenched as he hunched over. His ulcer was kicking up and he needed some Maalox.

Once, during the early days of the AIDS epidemic, I had seen Mary grab one of these reluctant fathers and shake him by the shoulders.

"That's your little boy up there, you stupid son-of-abitch!" she shouted with anguish in her voice. *"Your little boy*! Don't matter how he got sick. Don't matter what's killin' him. He's dying and he needs you. He needs his daddy. So get your ass up there—*Now!"*

It took two orderlies to calm Mary down, but in the end the father went upstairs to his son. I've often felt the same way about the men who could not accept their sons' homosexuality. They were frightened about something they didn't understand and couldn't comprehend. How could their little boy, whom they had loved and been proud of, be gay? Their sense of betrayal eclipsed their love, and time was running out.

Stan and Sally went downstairs to talk and have a cup of coffee. I sat with James.

"What would you say to him if he did come upstairs?" I asked.

"I'd say I'm sorry I caused him such pain. I know how much he's hurting. He's always been so proud of me and now he thinks I've failed him." James cried quietly.

"Because you're gay?" I asked.

"Yes. And because I have AIDS. Good boys, even good gay boys, don't get AIDS." He forced a smile. "Right?"

"I don't believe that any more than you do," I replied.

"Yeah, but he does. And he hates me for it. He thinks I'm dirt and he can't wait to sweep me under the rug."

"Don't you think you're being a little harsh?" I asked.

"And what he's doing isn't harsh?"

"What else would you tell him?"

"I'd tell him that I'm the same person I've always been. Nothing has changed. I've always loved him and I love him now, even when he's breaking my heart. I need him to accept the fact that I'm gay. I need him to love me. And hold me. And to forgive me for dying."

I sat on the side of his bed and took James in my arms and held him while he cried.

Downstairs, his father ground out another cigarette and leafed through a dog-eared copy of *Time*. Sally sat next to him and tried to get him to come upstairs, but still he refused. After a while she came back upstairs and asked me if I'd go down and talk to him.

"Maybe he'll listen to you, Ted. I don't know what to say to him anymore. He just shuts me out." She took my hand in hers. "Please."

I went downstairs and found James, Sr. I was surprised how much the father and the son looked alike. I introduced myself, we shook hands, and I sat down. He lit another cigarette and glared at me.

"What would you say to James if you weren't so angry with him?"

"What's that supposed to mean?" he asked, frowning.

"Well, you are angry with him, aren't you? Angry that he's gay, that he has AIDS, that he waited so long to tell you.

Perhaps you're angry and disappointed that he didn't trust you or your love enough to give you some time to understand."

"Who the hell understands queers?" he snapped.

"I wasn't talking about queers. I was talking about your son, James, Jr. The one who looks like you and always wanted to be like you. The one who loves you and wants and needs your love. You know, that little kid you taught to swim and to play ball. The one you helped with his homework. The one you carried in your arms to the emergency room when he fell out of a tree. The one you bought an old car for when he was 18 and then helped him fix up every night when you got home from work. That kid. Your son."

I watched him clench his fists.

"*Shut up*! That kid doesn't exist anymore. He's dead. He killed him."

"No, he's not dead. Not yet. But he will be soon. Maybe a few days, maybe a few hours. And when he dies you'll have the rest of your life to figure out why you were such a spineless coward who didn't have the guts—the balls—to go to him and say goodbye. You're one hell of a real man. What I can't figure out is why your son loves you so much."

I rose and headed for the elevator.

"Wait!" called James's father. "What. . .what can I say to him? I've been trying to think of what to say to him."

"Would you know what to say to him if he wasn't gay?" I asked. "If he wasn't dying of AIDS?"

"Maybe. Yes. Yes, then he'd be my son and not some stranger that I don't—can't—understand."

I put my hand on his shoulder.

"I'm going to go upstairs and get Sally and Stan and send them home. Then I'll arrange for you to stay here as long as it takes. But sometime between now and tomorrow morning when they come back, I hope you'll find the courage to go upstairs and say goodbye to your son. I can't tell you what to say or how to find a way to say it, but if you don't say it, I'll come back and kick your ass.

"James, Sr., you remind me of my father. We look alike, too, and it's always difficult for us to face each other. I see in him what I'm slowly becoming and he sees in me everything he used to be. The older I get, the more like him I seem to become. And the more I become like him, the angrier he gets that I didn't learn from his mistakes."

James softened a little. His fists unclenched and he allowed himself to smile.

"You feel the same way about James, Jr.," I continued. "You always wanted it to be better, easier, for him, and now you know it won't be. But, it can be if you give him back your love."

Sometime during the night James, Sr., went upstairs to see his son. Their fear and anger were mirrored in one another's faces. Each struggled to overcome his anger. In part they succeeded, but mostly they failed. These troubled waters were not so easily calmed. Perhaps, in time, they would have come to an understanding. But for the last three days of his life, James had his father by his side. It was more than many others had had.

The closing between James and his father was only partial. Honoring and remembrance of the dead is an essential part of closing for the one left behind.

When James felt his own death approaching he began to plan how he wanted to close with his parents and with Stan. Since his father would not see or speak to him, James planned how he wanted to say goodbye to Stan and his mother.

They settled the matter of his estate and the scattering of his ashes. Then they spent a week doing favorite things together and having pictures taken. The last night of the closing week the three went to dinner and then walked hand-in-hand through the park and talked quietly about the meaning of their lives together.

James, Sr., had enabled his son to close and to die in peace, but for the father there were darker days ahead.

Like many others, James's father would have to begin the long journey from guilt to commemoration. Only then would he find his own peace. Whatever those final moments between father and son consisted of, they were not enough for James, Sr.

Shortly after midnight, six months after James died, I

turned off the late news and answered the demanding ringing of my phone.

"Mr. Menten, it's James's father."

"How are you?" I asked.

"Not so good. Could I come and see you?" His voice quavered.

"Sure. When?"

"As soon as possible. . .please."

"I have a fathers' group tomorrow night. Would you like to join us?" No response. "We could get together before the group and have a cup of coffee together. How's that?"

"Yes. That would be fine. Thank you, Mr. Menten."

He looked 10 years older and my guess was that he'd been drinking—and not just today. His jaw still had that determined set to it but his eyes were red-rimmed and he seemed almost on the verge of tears. I offered him coffee or something stronger. He smiled and asked if he could have one and then the other. He needed a jump-start. I knew the feeling.

For an hour I listened as he described his misery. He felt guilty, anguished, and, at times, suicidal. He was sure Sally hated him. She and Stan went out and left him alone with his sorrow and recriminations. He felt he was a failure as a father and he still didn't understand about his son being homosexual. Having neither comfort nor understanding, he wasn't sleeping, he was drinking on and off the job. He was haunted by thoughts of James, how much he loved him, how much he missed him.

"Remember you told me that James and I were like you and your father?" he smiled momentarily and then looked away. "You said the apple didn't fall far from the tree. Well, without James I feel as empty as a tree in winter."

And then there was that terrible silence where I was supposed to say the right thing that would stop his pain. Except those words don't exist.

"Would you like to sit in with the group?" I responded. "You won't have to say anything. Just listen." He nodded and I refilled his coffee cup.

"I'll go and set up. We'll start in about 10 minutes." He sipped his coffee and looked into space.

"OK, guys, let's settle down. Say hello to my friend, James. His son, James, Jr., died six months ago and I'll bet that not one of you can guess why he's here."

"He couldn't say goodbye," they chimed in unison. James looked down at his shoes.

As the weeks passed, James, Sr., became a regular member of the fathers' group. He wrote letters to his son. First angry letters, then why letters, then letters asking for forgiveness and love. They helped a little, but his main support came from the other fathers.

"That kid of mine really pissed me off." Joe, an

accountant, was speaking. "He was always giving me this gay pride stuff. I mean it was bad enough he was queer—but proud? That really burned me up. And, of course, his mother thought it was just fine. She even marched with him in the Gay Pride parade." His voice drops. "The thing is, now I wish I had."

"Yeah," says Albert. "At least your son stayed a man. My kid was a drag queen. When he was a little kid he used to dress up and we all thought it was funny, but then he wanted to do it all the time. I couldn't take it so I threw him out of the house. He was only 15. My wife left me for six months. She returned only when I let him come back home. I was embarrassed all the time. He kept winning all these trophies. Now I look at them and it breaks my heart. Why the hell couldn't they be football trophies?"

The fathers write letters and take turns reading them aloud. Then we work on the quilts. Many people who have lost someone they love to AIDS make a quilt panel to remember them by. The panels are gathered by The Names Project and are displayed around the country. The quilt gets larger every day.

Most of these men have never even sewn a button on a shirt, so I give a quick course in needle threading and off they go.

I think most men like to work with their hands. They seem to open up more easily if they're busy working rather than sitting around just talking. At any rate, the quilting time is a lot less intense and soul searching. There's even time for humor.

"One night," says Albert, "I'm watchin' the game on TV and all these cheerleaders come out and start shakin' their stuff. I start to thinkin' my Bobby could have done that. He could have been a cheerleader and shaken his stuff just as good as any of them. I got the trophies to prove it!"

After a few weeks James, Sr. joined AA and stopped drinking. He went to dinner with Sally and Stan, and then one night with Stan alone. Then they all marched together in a Gay Pride parade.

And all of us—the fathers and the mothers and the sisters and the brothers and the lovers—went to Washington, D.C., to see the Names Project quilt.

Now, sewn together with thousands of others was the quilt panel that James, Sr., had created to honor his son. We had spent weeks designing it, cutting the fabric, and stitching it together. The cloth wasn't always cut evenly and the stitches were irregular but strong. There was a certain boldness about the design that seemed born of struggle.

The panel shows two bright red apples side by side. Over the apples was James, Jr.'s full name, and beneath the apples, in large block letters, were the words his father had painstakingly cut and sewn:

BELOVED SON • GAY AND PROUD

Simplicity

I met James, Jr., at the closing ceremony for Thomas. Stan and James and Thomas were members of my People with AIDS Harmony group. Together we had planned Thomas's closing.

Thomas was a man who loved formality almost as much as he enjoyed laughter. I remember thinking that his life, or more accurately, his style, was summed up in a photograph I had seen of him wearing a tuxedo, holding a slim champagne glass, his head thrown back in a hearty laugh.

His closing was to be an affirmation of his love for Les, his partner of 14 years, his friends, and family. We were assembled in a private room of his favorite restaurant, enjoying good food and drink. Thomas circulated among us like a gentle breeze. He seemed to be everywhere at once and finally, after dinner, we settled down and the ceremony began.

Thomas gave a moving speech, expressing his love for everyone in the room. Afterward, we were called up, one by one, to receive our remembrance.

Thomas had decided to give each person he loved a special memento of himself. He had gone through the treasure trove of his possessions and selected an item for each of us. He had also taken his favorite photograph of himself and had copies made and framed. Each frame was inscribed with a personal thought. These two items were his legacy of love. When we had received Thomas's gift, hugged him, and sat down, he turned to Les and reaffirmed his devotion.

Then we all drank too much.

A Place of One's Own

Many patients are confined to their beds and will never again leave the hospital. Trapped inside a 12×12 space painted an efficient/innocuous shade of green, they go from moment to moment, hour to hour, day to day, with little or no variation in routine. Often they are connected to life-support equipment or an IV which prevents them from leaving their beds. With some imagination, a dreary hospital room can be transformed into a more cheerful place.

A few flowers in a vase isn't a garden, so Sophia made dozens of tissue-paper blossoms to fill Stanley's room.

David covered the walls of William's room with movie posters recalling all their favorite films. He bought dozens of glossy publicity photographs of movie stars and wrote outrageous messages "from the stars" across the bottom.

Brenda filled her daughter's room with stuffed toys so that when Susie woke up she thought she was in a toy store.

Maryanne was a frustrated interior decorator before she developed cancer. Her husband brought her all the latest

decorating magazines and about 20 floral print bed sheets.
Maryanne turned the sheets into drapes, swags, table covers,
and chair covers. Giant fabric bows were tied everywhere,
including the base of her IV stand.

Most elaborate of all, Vito took his darling Serena to
Rome. They had always wanted to go to Italy to visit the home
of their parents, but then Serena had contracted AIDS. Vito
covered her walls with posters that he begged, borrowed, and
stole from travel agencies. He even brought a large,
freestanding Tower of Pisa made of cardboard.

One night Vito hired an Italian accordionist and a
violinist to serenade his wife. He stuck candles into Chianti
bottles, covered her dinner tray with a red-checked cloth, and
rented *Three Coins in the Fountain* and *Roman Holiday*, Serena's
favorite films.

Vito even staged a grape-crushing festival, which
consisted of mashing grapes in a wooden bucket with his fists.

After Serena died, Vito took her ashes to Italy and
scattered them from a gondola in Venice. But first he and
Serena visited every place they had dreamed of going. I
received postcards from both of them as they traveled.

A few days after Vito scattered Serena's ashes, I
received a postcard of St. Mark's Square. It showed the famous
moment when the bells ring and thousands of pigeons fly
skyward. On the back was written "Ciao, Ted—Serena."

Goodbye, Serena.

Warning Signs

Every day, suicides seem to come without warning, devastating those left behind. But even these unexpected suicides are preceded by telltale signs. These signs are a kind of closing, but we may not recognize them.

After years of battling a drug addiction, Greg went into a rehab program and emerged clean and sober. A few months later he was using drugs again, and he went into another program. Again he came out clean and sober. And again he started using. He finally entered an ongoing program that seemed to be helping. His life appeared to be on the upswing.

During the next few months he told me how well he was doing. He seemed to have a real hold on his life.

One night he showed up at my house. He said he was passing through town and thought he'd stop by and say hi. He looked great—healthy and vibrant and full of cheer. We talked for hours and he thanked me for pushing him into rehab and standing by him as a friend. He was back at work and loving it.

Here before me was a bright, happy, young man with

his life ahead of him and the world at his feet. This was the friend I had known years ago, before the nightmare of drugs.

For months I had worried that my pressuring him into a rehab program had been a kind of rejection. At first I resisted the tough-love philosophy, but finally realized that to really be his friend I had to take a stand, no matter how painful. Now I felt relief. Greg had taken the time to stop by and share his happiness with me. He had forgiven me for taking a stand against his habit. His victory was mine, and I rejoiced with him.

At the end of the evening he hugged me and, as he walked away, he turned and waved goodbye—a big, happy smile on his face. A week later he took his life.

Greg's visit was a closing. His gift to me was his forgiveness. He wanted me to remember him the way he was that night, the way he had been when we had met years before.

Yes, he'd been passing through town—on a drug run. He was still hooked and I suspect that he felt there would never be an end to it. So he decided to end the pain himself.

Perhaps if I had been more astute I would have recognized that this was a common pattern of potential suicides. The knowledge of impending death—even self-inflicted death—produces a need to close. It is with sadness that I realize that Greg's closing was complete. Even though I was unaware that I was closing with him, I had, indeed, closed. All I now remember are the good times and my happy, smiling friend waving goodbye.

Make a Memory

In 1984, I found a book entitled *Let's Make a Memory* by Gloria Gaither and Shirley Dobson. The subtitle of the book is: "Great Ideas for Building Family Traditions and Togetherness."

The book is filled with more than 200 pages of ideas about how to make things special, very special, and even more special (like sneaking into the kids' room on Christmas morn and taking a snapshot of them waking up). It is filled with delightful, loving ways for a family to share experiences. It has a brief chapter on dealing with illness, and some of those ideas are great. But more than that, the book suggests many ideas that can be adapted to the process of closing.

The simple but loving projects include making a home video to share with the loved one who is confined to the hospital; scrapbooks; memory books; and my favorite, the tree of love. This is a potted plant with notes from friends and family tied to the branches. The same theme is carried out with a basket of gifts from friends and neighbors or school chums.

Sick people spend a lot of time alone and a video or a scrapbook that they can go back to again and again is very comforting. When I'm working with terminal patients, I try to involve them in ongoing projects, like the never-ending Button and Blossom story. When a kid goes home or becomes an outpatient, I continue the tale through ongoing letters. If the child has to return to the hospital, he or she is still up-to-date with the adventures.

Facing the death of a loved one is never, ever easy. But there are ways to soften the blow and to make sure that everyone gets a chance to say I love you before saying goodbye.

Little Mary is 80 years old and stands about five feet tall. She has cancer and fallen arches. Of the two, she complains most about the arches. We met in the sunroom one afternoon when she asked me if I had a bear to spare. I asked her why she wanted one of my bears; the way I heard it she got plenty of hugs from every fella she could get one from.

"Getting hugged is good for morale. I used to hug soldiers and sailors at the USO during both wars. First as a tootsie and then as a granny." Mary laughs and grabs my cheek and pinches it. "Gimme a bear, you old smoothie, or I'll start rumors about us."

I brought her a bear the next day. It was a payoff to keep the rumors from flying—my reputation was bad enough.

"I'm gonna make this bear a miracle scarf," Mary

declared. "I'm gonna knit one inch in a different color every day I'm alive. It'll be like Joseph's coat of many colors. It'll drive those doctors crazy because they keep telling me I haven't got more than a week or two. It'll bust their chops when this bear and I prance into their examining rooms with his scarf dragging miles and miles behind him. Nice touch, don't you think?"

"You're pretty sassy, Mary. And mean enough to outlive us all. Heaven won't be the same when you get there."

"That's the truth," she said, beaming. "They don't make old broads like me nowadays."

"Well, Mary, it took 80 years to get you this perfect."

"Don't sweet-talk me, Mr. Silly, I know all about you. Now shoo and bring me some pretty colored yarn the next time you're back this way. Scoot—your kids are calling."

They told Little Mary she had a few weeks and then they told her she had a few more. She just laughed and went on knitting her miracle—one colorful inch for every colorful day.

The afternoon breeze blows through my room where I sit typing. A few papers rustle and I look up at him, that bear with the rainbow scarf wrapped around and around and around his neck. One of the scarf's long, multicolored tails lifts gently in the breeze and seems to be waving at me.

When the box arrived I took him out and measured the scarf. Two hundred and twenty-one inches of miracle—one colorful day at a time.

I don't remember the first time I heard the term *closing,* but I do remember the first time I didn't experience it.

My mother had been in poor health for a number of years and the doctors seemed unable to pin down the reason. So she went from doctor to doctor, treatment to treatment, with little success. She had no energy, she couldn't maintain her weight, and she was disheartened by it all.

My folks' home is in Florida, and I live in New York, so we keep in touch mostly by phone. When my dad called to say that mother was in the hospital, I wasn't surprised or alarmed because he seemed calm enough. I asked if he wanted me to fly down. He replied that if I did, my mother might think she was sicker than she was. I believe he thought he was doing the right thing and I accepted his judgment. A few days later he called to say that mom had taken a terrible turn and was slipping fast. I was on the next flight to Florida.

I was shocked by how frail my mother looked. The

hospital room, filled with life-support equipment, was hardly a cheerful atmosphere. She was in and out of consciousness but she never again knew who I was or why I was there. We never talked again; we never laughed together again. We never said goodbye. It takes two to say goodbye, and my mother was unable to say goodbye to her only child.

Many religions offer a closing ritual which comes some time after the actual death and burial. For example, Jews wait one year before placing a headstone on the grave.

In more recent years, new-age thinking has given rise to a variety of memorial services ranging from the scattering of ashes to testimonial gatherings where loved ones stand and share a remembrance, and in so doing, they extend that blessing to others.

The AIDS epidemic has produced two distinct forms of memorial. First, the Names Project Quilt, which is so powerful it knocks the breath out of you. Its enormous size is testament to the number of lives lost to the disease. The sight of the thousands of lovingly handmade panels is profound and overwhelming.

The second memorial is almost as profound in its simplicity. A group of men and women gather together to recall and share the experience of knowing someone who has died of AIDS. They stand in a circle in a clearing or a park and each holds a string attached to a pure white balloon. After sharing the blessing of his or her remembrance, each person says goodbye and releases the balloon as a symbol of letting go and as a symbol of the spirit's ascension.

This ceremony, as well as many others, allows the individual to share a personal closing with people who are united by their love of the one who is gone.

Whether it is the family gathered together to place an honoring headstone, or a group joined over a candlelit dinner to swap stories about their friend, or friends, family, and lovers gathered in an open field to let go of their balloons, the process of mutual closing can be a joyous and healing experience.

Those with the knowledge of death are like the couples standing together in the railroad station who take time to embrace and say goodbye. But when death comes suddenly, without warning, then the ones left behind may feel rage and helplessness, unable to hold their loved one a final time and say, "I love you."

Still, there are ways to say goodbye even after the train has left the station. These are the stories of people who found a way to finally close with a loved one who left without having time to say goodbye. With letters and songs and strolls down memory lane, they reached past death to touch the one they loved.

Slowly, and with determination, they made the journey alone from bewilderment and sorrow to honoring and closing. And finally they found the blessing of remembrance.

The Viking Fire

In the film *Rocket Gibraltar*, a grandfather, played majestically by Burt Lancaster, assembles his children and grandchildren at his summer home. He knows that he is dying, perhaps not in the actual sense, but in the general way that all of us who have passed the halfway mark become aware of our mortality.

His children, caught up in their own lives and problems, tend to ignore him. The only ears he can find to listen to him are those of his grandchildren. He confides to the youngsters that when he dies he wants to be buried like a Viking, at sea in a flaming boat. He fills the children's minds with heroic images and tales of the Viking heaven where good men go if the sunset and the boat's flames merge and become one.

When he dies, the children take his body away without telling their parents what has happened. They build a Viking boat from an old rowboat and use a painted bed sheet for a sail. Then they put their grandfather's body lovingly on a pyre of twigs. Not for one moment do they question the rightness, the correctness, of what they are doing. Despite a last-minute attempt by the parents to intervene, the children set the ship adrift and shoot flaming arrows into the pyre.

In the final moments of the film we see the children and their parents standing together, watching the flames of the ship merging with the sunset as the soul of their father and grandfather sails on to Valhalla.

The entire film is a hymn to closing and to the innocence and wonder of children. Too often, as adults, we fail to listen with the innocence that children do. Those we love are trying to tell us how they want to die, how they want to be buried, and how they want to be honored and remembered.

Franklin Roosevelt led this nation victoriously through a global war. Before he died, he requested only the simplest of services. His wishes were completely ignored; he was instead given a ceremony that rivaled the funerals of kings. The explanation given for this disrespectful breach of trust was that the nation needed a great funeral to express their grief and to honor their leader.

If we truly honor those we love, we will listen to their wishes, even if we do not agree with them. An important aspect of closing is accepting that death is near, whispering into the ear of our loved one. No matter how difficult it may be for us to accept, we need to acknowledge that our loved one is preparing to take the journey. In loving kindness we should help him or her get ready.

Among the Missing

At the end of the Vietnam conflict the soldiers returned home and tried to resume normal lives. Months later the nation began to hear a new phrase: MIA— Missing in Action. A second wave of grief rolled over the country as it was revealed that hundreds, possibly thousands, of sons, husbands, and fathers remained unaccounted for.

As time passed, the grieving turned to rage. And even today the problem continues. Not knowing is always worse than knowing.

Every year thousands of children simply vanish without a trace. Possibly injured, kidnapped, or murdered, these missing children may be found in a few days, weeks, months, or even years. But until they are found, alive or dead, they are unaccounted for.

After a period of time, different for each individual, there must begin the process of closing. But, unlike a closing with someone who is dying or who has already died, this closing has a catch. The door must remain partly open.

If those who are left behind cannot close, they will spend the rest of their lives waiting for the return that may never come. That is a long time to be in pain.

This kind of grieving is different from the grief felt for a loved one who has died. When we know that death has come we can, in time, let go and find peace of mind by accepting that our loved one is at peace.

But that gentle closing is denied to those of us with missing loved ones. The thing we fear most is that our loved one is not at peace, but may actually be in danger. To even suggest that we say goodbye feels as if we're turning our backs. No, saying goodbye is not possible. We cling to hope, to the slimmest possible chance of survival.

Weeks pass into years, and still that hope remains. But as time passes that slim thread of hope becomes stretched to the limit and all the heartache must somehow be eased. The process of closing, of letting go, must occur. Some will choose, after a while, to believe that death has come and begin the process of closing and mourning.

Others, like Rachael, will never be able to say goodbye.

"When Cindy disappeared 10 years ago I thought they would find her in a few hours. Days at most. But it dragged on and on—all the false starts, rumors, anonymous tips, crank calls. The whole range of craziness that surrounds a child's disappearance. We had enough clues to find a hundred little girls. Sightings for another hundred. I just couldn't let go, I became obsessed with finding Cindy.

"After five years my husband left because I had pulled so far away from him. I pushed him away because he tried to comfort me. He wanted me to heal but I kept pulling the wound open again. I needed the pain to keep going, to keep believing. I'm still obsessed. She's my baby and until they can prove otherwise, she is still alive."

"How do you handle it now, after 10 years?" I ask.

"Not much better than I did the first night. I still cry. I still imagine that I see her. I still talk about her in the present tense. I'm keeping her alive. But after the initial shock and the lingering hope, I knew that everyone around me was losing faith, including my husband. So I started writing letters to Cindy. One a day, every day. I tell her how much I love her and miss her. I tell her what we're doing to find her. I tell her about what's going on around here. I tell her what I want for her as she grows up.

"When she does come home she'll have a lot of reading to catch up on. Last year I started making tapes because now that I'm getting older I worry that something might happen to me. I want her to know the sound of my voice. I have a nice picture of myself taken every year so she can watch me get older."

"Do you ever feel like you need to say goodbye to her and let go?" I watch her reaction. She is very calm.

"No, I never do. But I do say goodnight at the end of every day. That's a one-day-at-a-time kind of closing. And I leave the porch light on, that's a beacon. And I thank God for another day. And just before I go to sleep, I think—maybe tomorrow."

Rachael's faith and determination are the basis of her strength. There is the strength that comes from accepting, and there is the strength that comes from believing. To survive, we must believe that what we believe is right. Closing is not always saying goodbye. Closing can also mean saying goodnight.

Untie the Yellow Ribbon

When U.S. troops were shipped to Kuwait, families left behind marked their loved ones' absence with yellow ribbons. These yellow bows, blossoming like crocuses in spring, were tied everywhere, including around the traditional old oak tree.

When the troops came home, the ribbons were untied. For most of us the war is over, but for those who have lost someone, it rages on. Because not everyone will accept the finality of death, some ribbons remain, fading, but still tightly tied around the heart.

From the story of the prodigal son, to Holocaust survivors, to the return of lost children, we celebrate that which was lost and is found, and that which we thought was dead but is alive.

The miracle of return. The miracle of coming home.

When death comes and we see it happen, it is real. When death comes and we are told about it, but do not see it, it is less real. And if death is only suspected but not confirmed, as in the case of the lost child or the missing soldier, it is not real at all and the ribbon stays tightly knotted.

When death is unconfirmed it is natural to go on hoping for the miracle of return. But there is a point at which the beauty of hope turns into the lie of denial.

At one time or other everyone facing death, either their own or a loved one's, goes through denial. It is natural, even helpful. Faced with the knowledge of death, we fight harder if we deny it a little. Denial gives us breathing space and some time to work our way to acceptance.

But some people continue to deny the death of a loved one even in the face of absolute evidence. They cheat death by not going to the hospital. Or by not going to the cemetery, or the funeral, or the memorial service. They tighten the ribbon and deny. They indulge in the fantasy of the miracle of return. They see their loved one everywhere, like the fans who see James Dean pumping gas in Texas, or Elvis at the fast-food restaurant.

Robert's wife was lost at sea in a boating accident. They were 12 miles from land when she fell overboard and was swept under before anyone knew what had happened. The coast guard searched for hours, but Wendy's body was never recovered.

That was 10 years ago. Last year Robert saw Wendy at the mall and followed her for two hours. She was wearing the same blue shirt and blue hair ribbon she had on the day she was lost. The month before, Robert had seen her on Wall Street, and before that in California, and before that...and that...and that....

Robert's sightings are no different from a thousand others.

If we are ever to move forward out of denial and into honoring and remembrance, then we must untie the yellow ribbon and throw it away or, as part of the honoring, press it in our Bible or family album. Until we do that we have not completed our closing and have not really said goodbye.

Miracles happen, and when they do they are inspiring. But we must not confuse real miracles with false, imaginary, or wished-for ones. Part of letting go is giving up the false miracle.

After Robert finally was able to untie his yellow ribbon, I suggested that he replace it with a blue one to match the ribbon Wendy had worn. Now when he sees a young woman wearing a blue ribbon he remembers Wendy, her hair tied back, standing in the wind, laughing. He honors their love by letting Wendy go, by saying goodbye. In return, he gets the blessing of remembrance neatly tied in a bright blue ribbon.

The Sleeping Princess

This is a fairy tale without an ending, at least for the moment.

Once upon a time in a faraway kingdom, a princess fell into a coma. Knights and princes from around the world came and tried to awaken her with a kiss. All failed. Finally a prince from the edge of the world came to see the slumbering princess. Her beauty was beyond belief and he instantly fell in love with her. He loved her more than anything in heaven and on earth. As he leaned over to press his lips against hers, the whole kingdom held its breath.

Nothing happened. He kissed her again, yet still she slept. In frantic desperation, he seized her by the shoulders and shook her. He shouted at her to awaken, but her eyes remained closed.

Closing with a loved one who has gone into coma is even more difficult than closing with someone who is missing. The loved one who is in coma is missing, too. She is, quite simply, not there. As with the prolonged grief for the missing to return, the wait for the one in coma to awaken may take an entire lifetime.

Closing should be an act of love, a celebration of all that is and was good between the one who is leaving and the one who must remain behind. But how can you let go when there is a chance, no matter how slim, that your loved one may return, might awaken? It has happened. There is hope. And there is also the pain of hope.

I thought about the parents of the sleeping princess and wondered what I would have said to them. Would I have suggested that they think of her as dead, and to mourn her, close with her, let go and try to carry on? I don't think so.

Would I have suggested that they continue living with their pain while they searched for a prince who could miraculously awaken her? I think not.

Would I suggest that they continue to care for her? Yes. Would I suggest that they hope for a blessing? Yes. Would I suggest that they stop feeling responsible and therefore guilty? Yes. Would I suggest that they say goodbye? No.

If I were her father, the king, I would sit by her side each evening and hold her hand. I would marvel at the princess's beauty. I would think how much like her mother, the queen, she was. I would recall her laughter and the thousand joys she had given me before she slumbered. I would tell her of my adventures and my dreams, knowing she would keep and cherish them in her silence. And I'm sure I would weep because that seems like the natural thing to do. I would promise to love and protect her just as I did her mother. And then I would kiss her gently and take a moment to memorize her beauty. Then I would let go for today. I would say "Goodnight. Sweet dreams."

A few weeks ago, one of my patients slipped into coma. The coma patient's family and I organized round-the-clock vigils. Someone would always be in Susan's room, talking constantly to her. If we left the room we put the TV or the radio on. We read books until we were hoarse. We told stories, sang songs, told bad jokes, and kept in voice contact with the slumbering princess.

After two weeks we were worn out, but we kept on. Steven, Susan's twin brother, was with her when she awakened. He had been talking all night about the year they entered high school and how difficult it had been for them to be separated. He mused on and on, his voice getting more fatigued by the minute. He gulped water and continued with the story. As he stopped to take another sip, his sister suddenly said: "Will you please shut up."

The Truth About Why

Most kids want to know why the earth is round or if there really is a man in the moon. Kids with life-threatening illnesses want to know those things, too, but they have another question: "Why am I going to die?"

When George Leigh Mallory was asked why he wanted to climb Mount Everest, he replied: "Because it is there."

I like that answer and I thought about it in terms of the other question. Just as a mountain is climbed because it is *there*, people die because they *can*. It is basic to the concept of being alive.

Accepting death is essential to coming to terms with the loss we feel. While death is never easy to accept, we can often find comfort when it is put into perspective. We say that Grandma had a long and rewarding life, that Johnny died a hero, that peace has come at last to the one we love who has been suffering. By putting death into context, we comfort ourselves.

The death of a child is more difficult. Often there seems to be no way to gain perspective on a child's life ending.

Robert and Linda's son, Robert Jr., died after a long struggle with leukemia. The entire time Bobby had been sick his father had been a rock of strength, while Linda seemed always on the brink of desperation.

At the funeral, Robert had stood tall and strong, while Linda clung to his arm, crying. In the months that followed, she sat and mourned while Robert went to work and acted as though everything had returned to normal. It seemed to Linda that he was made of stone, that he felt nothing.

Then, six months after Bobby's death, Robert came home early from the office and started to cry. He lay on the floor, curled in the fetal position, sobbing uncontrollably. Linda tried to comfort him but he didn't even seem to know she was there. After several hours she called their doctor. He told her that it was a delayed stress reaction, common in men. But Robert was still on the floor the next morning, and he stayed there until it was dark again outside. Linda stayed with him, but nothing she said seemed to console him. He was beyond her reach.

Now, sitting together in their living room just three days later, Robert looks haggard and seems to have aged years since I had last seen him. He huddles in his chair, his body closing into itself. His eyes are misty, unfocused. Linda and I talk quietly but Robert seems off in his own world. I ask Linda to let us talk alone.

Slowly at first, Robert opens up and talks about what

he is feeling: pain, rage, and frustration. These are familiar words from men who feel they must appear strong for their families and on the job while carrying all the suffering inside. Many women must do the same thing, but in our culture we accept the idea that even a strong woman can collapse under the pressure of grief. But not strong men. Robert felt terribly alone in his misery. He had cut himself off because he thought he had to.

"Robert," I ask, "why didn't you share your pain with Linda?"

"Showing her my pain wouldn't have stopped hers."

"Maybe not, but right now she can help you stop yours. If you let her. If you share your pain with her now, she can be your strong partner just as you were hers. Right now you are both alone in your grief and each of you will grieve in your own personal way, but you can do it *together*. You can be alone *together* and, in time, you'll both be stronger for it."

In the months that followed, Linda and Robert shared their progress. Linda spoke first.

"We still can't understand why Bobby had to die. It just doesn't make sense. We try to understand, but we just haven't gotten to that point yet. Maybe we never will."

"When I was a kid," I confided to them, "I thought my father was the smartest person in the world until I asked him why the light went on when I flipped the switch. He told me *how* but he couldn't explain *why*. He never could because 'why' is almost always an act of faith. Faith in God, or faith in yourself, or faith in the process. We simply believe that when we flip the switch, the light will go on. Some people will never even care why, but I suspect that I always will.

"And I suspect that we will always wonder why children die. We all think that kids should grow up and lead full lives. That's what we expect because most of the time that's the way it is. So when children die it doesn't seem fair. But children, being alive, can also die. As difficult as it is to understand, it is also that simple. So we must accept it and begin to heal."

It is not possible to offer an answer to the question of why. But it is enough to acknowledge the constant truth of the question.

Some medicine cannot cure, but it can soothe.

Sentenced to Life

This is the nightmare: A black-robed judge strikes his gavel and calls the courtroom to order. The defendant rises as the judge, his brow furrowed, renders his verdict. "You are hereby sentenced to imprisonment of life."

In the defendants' seat, the widow screams, "No!" Jeanne sits up in her bed, trembling. She is drenched in perspiration, her heart is pounding, her temples throb, and her tears begin again.

Jeanne brings me lemonade and we walk to the edge of the garden and sit on the glider. Jeanne is 25. Her husband, Leon, was 28 when he died suddenly last year. They had been married less than a year.

Sipping her drink, Jeanne recalls her husband. "We never disagreed about anything." She smiles. "It was almost boring, but there was a funny kind of security in it, too. I guess we weren't really looking for excitement. We both liked things calm. Leon was incredibly gentle. He touched everything as though it was precious." The smile fades. "These nightmares are driving me crazy."

"What do you think they mean?" I ask.

"In the dream the accused, me, is sentenced to imprisonment of life. The first few times I had the dream I thought the judge was giving the usual sentence of imprisonment for life. The third or fourth time I realized that the sentence was not just imprisonment. It was imprisonment *in life*. Life was my prison. That's when I really became frightened. Now, each time I have the dream I wake up more and more frightened."

She looks toward the house and bites her lower lip, trying to hold back her tears. I lean over and take her hand. "It's OK, Jeanne, it's only a dream."

"No, it's my punishment."

"Because you're alive."

"Yes."

Millions died in the Nazi death camps. Many of those who survived carried the guilt of having survived. When Job asked God "Why me?" it was because he felt overly tested. When a survivor asks "Why me?" she feels overly blessed. Guilty of life.

Only on very rare occasions do we see death as a blessing. When it comes, bringing peace to a loved one who is suffering, we are able to see its virtue. But otherwise death is an intruder, interrupting life and its plans and dreams.

It takes a great deal of courage to think of death as a better place than life. Yet even though we fear death—the unknown place—we are curious about it. We may even be a little envious of our loved one who has gone ahead, leaving us with our pain.

"Jeanne," I say to her, "I want you to consider this. In your dream the judge sentences you to life—to living. Right now that is what frightens you because you can't imagine a life without Leon."

"No, I can't. I don't really want to," she replies.

"Hopefully, in time, you will commute your sentence and start a new life beyond the prison walls."

"You're telling me that there is life after Leon and I'm telling you that I can't—I won't—imagine that life."

She frowns and looks away from me.

"No, Jeanne, I'm telling you that there is life after Leon's death. I hope that you never stop loving him. I hope that you never stop honoring and remembering him. That you never lose the gift of your love and your life together. I hope that he will live forever in your heart because being forgotten is the only real death." I clasp her hands tightly in mine. "Stop asking 'why me' without listening to the answer."

"What is the answer?" she asks.

"I think you know the answer in your heart. Maybe you need to write Leon a letter and ask his advice, then sit quietly and listen for his answer. Maybe you should look into your heart and ask yourself what you would have wanted Leon to do with the rest of his life if it had been you who died.

"But I still feel guilty," she mutters.

"Do you think that's what Leon wants from you, expects from you?"

"No." Her lip trembles.

"What would Leon want?" I ask.

"My happiness."

"Then love and honor and remember him with that gift of your happiness."

"I'll try."

Closing doesn't mean shutting the door and turning away. Closing is the realization that there is life after the death of a loved one. It is in the form of memory, and it is the survivor's responsibility and honor to carry that memory while living life to the fullest.

From Sorrow to Remembrance

Perhaps the most difficult transition anyone has to make after the death of a loved one is the journey from grief and sorrow to remembrance and honoring. Our loss seems to overwhelm us and, fearing that we will dishonor the one we love by forgetting, we nurture grief, clinging to it with a desperation that comforts us.

But, in time, this grieving must give way to honoring and remembering. So often are the words "get on with your life" spoken to the one who is left behind, alone.

To move on is not to forget. It is to remember. It is to remember all that your loved one gave you, and all that you shared with your loved one. To move on is to celebrate those gifts and to know your loved one lives on in your memories. It is to realize how deeply he or she touched your life.

When I started working with terminal children I did not consider what it would mean to them when one of their friends died. Children experience the death of a loved one differently from adults. The concepts of grief, of honoring, of remembrance are too abstract for them. They understand only the pain of loss.

Here is a Button and Blossom story I tell the terminally ill children to teach them about remembrance.

• • •

Button and Blossom and the Sea of Tears

Button and Blossom sat on the beach and looked out across the ocean. The sun was setting and its golden light was reflected in the crystal tears that streamed down their cheeks. They could not speak because there were no words to say how sad they were and how much pain they felt. They had so loved Pony that when he died they had wanted to stop living as well.

The waves lap, lapped at the shore and tiny green sand crabs ran up and down the beach. Pink shells floated up in the sea foam and rested a few feet from where Button and Blossom sat. But all they saw was the darkness of their pain, and all they heard was the sound of their own tears.

"Hello!" cried a small voice from a distance. "Hello, hello, helloooooooooo!"

Button and Blossom looked up and saw a tiny sea horse bouncing up and down in the waves.

"Do you have a bucket?" cried the tiny voice.

"Yes," replied Button and Blossom together, for the moment forgetting their grief.

"Fill it with water and I will jump into it and come to

visit you on the shore."

Button and Blossom carried the red bucket to the water's edge and filled it with sea water. No sooner was it filled when the sea horse jumped in and splashed about. They ran back up the beach and put the bucket in the sand.

"Hello. My name is Jasper. Who are you?"

"I'm called Button and this is my sister, Blossom."

"How very, very pleasant to meet you. I don't get to meet many boys and girls under the sea. But I heard you crying and I thought I should come and see what the matter was." Jasper's bright black eyes rolled around in his head and he seemed to be looking at both children at the same time.

"Our friend Pony died," said Blossom, "and we are very sad."

"We miss him terribly," said Button. "He was a wonderful friend and things just won't be the same now that he's gone."

"That's what the King of the Ocean said," remarked Jasper with a knowing look. "Of course he wasn't always the King of the Ocean." Jasper ducked under the water for a moment to wet his throat, as he wasn't used to talking on dry land. "He used to be the King of the Hills and Valleys until his daughter died."

"Then what happened?" asked Button and Blossom curiously.

"Well, he cried, of course. He cried streams and then

rivers and then pools of tears. Nothing—absolutely nothing—comforted him. He kept weeping and weeping until the pools turned to lakes, and the lakes turned to seas. Pretty soon the land began to disappear under all his tears." Jasper rolled his eyes again and ducked under the water for a breath.

"When the Maker of All Things saw what was happening, he went to the King of Hills and Valleys and told him that enough was enough, and he should stop his crying." Jasper took a gulp of water and continued.

"Well, the King of Hills and Valleys stopped crying but his kingdom was already completely submerged, so that's how he became the King of the Ocean.

"The King was still sad about the loss of his beautiful daughter, so the Maker of All Things gave him a wonderful gift. Wanna know what it was?"

"Yes, yes," exclaimed Blossom and Button.

"The Maker of All Things gave the king a remembrance."

"A what?"

"A remembrance—a *remembrance* you ninnies. You know—beautiful things that would remind the king of his daughter."

"How?" asked Button.

"He made the ocean as blue as her eyes. And seashells as rosy pink as her cheeks. Coral as bright as her lips. And in the morning, when the sunlight filters through the water, it highlights the seaweed and shimmers like her hair. When the king saw all these things he felt close to his lovely daughter and he was never lonely again."

"But he would never hear her voice again," said Blossom.

"Oh, but he could," said Jasper. "When a brook babbles, that's her giggle. When the sea laps against the rocks, that's a tune she hums. She's all around him—in his remembrance."

"That's very nice, Jasper, but Pony was different. And I doubt that even the Maker of All Things could give us a remembrance of Pony."

"But he already has," exclaimed Jasper. "It's there, inside your head—forever. Close your eyes and you'll see Pony. If you listen to the wind, you'll hear him. If you truly, truly loved him he will always be there. That's the gift of remembrance that the Maker of All Things gives to those who love."

Button and Blossom sat on the beach with their eyes closed and their ears open. Soon they could hear Pony dashing toward them, the wind in his golden mane. Then they saw him dancing in the sunlight the way they loved him best. And then they knew that Pony would always be with them.

• • •

Dreams

Little Alice was hooked up to life support from the moment she was born. She lived only 14 days. Her parents, Barbara and Steve, came to see me because they couldn't stop the pain. They couldn't stop crying and they couldn't say goodbye. For two weeks they had waited for God to reach out and save little Alice; instead He had snatched her away, and they couldn't accept it. It wasn't fair. They had so many plans for her.

We sat together over cooling, untouched cups of coffee and I desperately wanted to help them but I didn't know how. I kept thinking about the saying that the answer is hidden inside the question.

"We used to lay in bed when I was pregnant and talk about her," began Barbara. "We knew it was a girl because I had to have the tests, you know, I'm 35.

"We waited until I had a good enough job so that we'd be secure. So we could give her all the good stuff we'd never had. Both of our families were kind of poor."

"All those plans we had," sighed Steve. They held each other's hands and tears streamed down their cheeks.

Inside the question is hidden the answer.

We sat there as the day faded into twilight. They had become lost in their pain while I was wandering around inside the question. Again and again their words came back to me ". . .we had so many plans."

"What plans?" I asked. They looked at me and then, slowly, they told me all about their hopes and dreams for little Alice.

"I wanted her to be Miss America. Beautiful and talented," admitted Steve.

Barbara smiled and touched Steve's cheek. "You men are all alike. You want a beautiful daughter but if some guy even looks at her you freak out."

They laughed and suddenly the solution was clear to me.

"Do it!" I exclaimed. "Give Alice everything you wanted to."

They looked at me like I was crazy.

"Look, as long as you keep feeling sorry that you can't give Alice all you wanted for her, you'll never be able to say goodbye to her. You'll always feel that you failed her. That you weren't the wonderful parents that you wanted to be. So I'm saying you should just go ahead and give her everything you wanted to give her."

"But we can't. She's. . ."

"In your hearts she's not."

Holding back their tears, they nodded their heads.

"OK, here's what you're going to do," I explained. "You're going to make a scrapbook of Alice's life. You're going to cut pictures out of magazines and write the captions from her birth until she gets married and goes off on her own. Everything you ever wanted for her—from perfect teeth to straight As and a bright red sports car—will go into the scrapbook. And when she gets married you'll take her in your arms and say goodbye. And you'll be at peace knowing that you've given her everything a daughter could want including perfect, loving parents. Then you will close the book and close with Alice."

Two years later I met the little girl that Barbara and Steve had adopted. They were laughing and playing together in the front yard.

"How's it going?" I asked.

"Just great," said Barbara. "You know, it's always easier with the second child."

"Yes," I said, smiling. "You did a wonderful job with Alice. Miss America, Olympic gold medalist, and now a prominent doctor. That's a tough act to follow.

"Do you think little Jean can measure up?"

"We'll just have to wait and see," laughed Steve. Come back in 18 years."

"It's a date."

Looking Back,
Moving Forward

They call themselves The Widows of Harmony. We have been getting together once a week to reconstruct. For a time, the widows wandered, bewildered, through the rubble that had once been a life shared with a partner. Alone, they rambled through the devastation, kicking up the dust of memory, fingering the artifacts of a past life.

"I just don't know who I am anymore." Jenny puts a white handkerchief to her eyes. "I mean, who am I now? The widow Harris? Who's that? I was Mrs. Thomas Harris for 33 years and now I don't know who I'm supposed to be. How I'm supposed to act."

"We need a guidebook," says Meg.

"Why don't you write one?" I ask.

"Oh, sure," replies Meg with a grin. "The blind leading the blind. I'm still in the middle of this maze. I haven't a clue where to go from here."

"You're further along than Jenny," I reply. "Tell Jenny how you got this far. Susan is several steps ahead of you, and if she turns and reaches back she can pull you forward. And if you turn back and reach for Jenny, you can pull her forward. It's a lifeline."

"OK," says Susan, "I'll start since I seem to be the one you think is furthest along." She sips her tea and settles back in her chair, remembering the day of destruction.

"Bill had a stroke. One minute he was there and the next he was gone. I was strong throughout everything because the kids needed me to be. And so, like mothers do, I put myself on hold. I held back the tears until much later—almost a year.

"Then I fell apart. I started dropping things on the floor and just leaving them there until, after a while, I had to step over them or kick them aside. I was slipping away into my grief and creating a death for myself. My kids got frightened and my doctor got concerned. My friends just got tired of me and my little death. So I ended up here."

Susan sips from her cup and continues. "Mostly, like the rest of you, I just sat here for the first few weeks, drinking my tea and nodding my head. It was all so familiar. It was everyone's song and we all knew the lyrics. And we had a little sing-along of grief. I used to call it The Widow's Chorus.

"One morning I woke up furious. Mad as hell. I threw a vase across the room and smashed it. It felt so good that I went downstairs and smashed every plate in the kitchen. Then I spent the day at Elizabeth Arden's. I got a total reconstruction and this blonde color I have now.

"Then I went out to the cemetery and visited Bill. I asked him what he thought of the new me and I got the feeling that he approved. But then I thought 'now what?' I called Ted. He said I should do something that would make me feel useful. So I volunteered at the hospital.

"I rocked babies, read to the old people and the ones who'd had eye surgery. I delivered magazines. And I did feel useful, but I didn't feel special. I guess I was a little envious of Ted—old Mister Silly here—because he did his thing. *His* thing. And deep inside was this longing to feel special again—the way Bill made me feel and my kids made me feel.

"So I started wondering what I could do that was different and would be all mine.

"At first I started a quilting class because I love making quilts, and that was good, but it finally didn't involve me enough. I knew it so well that it didn't challenge me. I had too much free time to slip back into my self-involvement and my grieving.

"One day I watched this elderly lady sitting in her wheelchair, looking intently out the window. I was curious about what held her attention so completely. Finally I realized that she was watching birds on a tree branch across the street. Suddenly I knew what it was that I could do. The next day I brought the woman a canary. She lit up like the Fourth of July."

Susan's eyes brighten as she tells her story. "Now I bring all sorts of pets to visit the patients in a dozen hospitals. I approached pet stores and asked them to donate pets. If they wouldn't donate them I asked for a discount. When that didn't work I'd ask for a loaner. Like a loaner car the garage gives you when yours is in for repairs. I get loaner parrots and loaner puppies and loaner gerbils. I'm busy all the time.

"Every week when I go to see Bill I have so much to tell him, so much to share with him. Sometimes I bring him a puppy, he loved puppies, and I let the puppy run around on his grave and I play with him, the way Bill would have.

"One day a patient called to me: 'Oh, petting lady. . .' and I knew she meant me. I was The Petting Lady. And that's where I am now. I'm a widow and a part of me will always be Mrs. William Stark. The widow Stark. But now I am also The Petting Lady and that is part of my healing, part of my personal reconstruction, part of my honoring.

"I have my gift of remembrance, and now I honor and share my new life with Bill. I still miss him terribly, but I'm moving forward and that's what's important."

Susan puts her teacup down and reaches her hand toward Meg, who in turn reaches for Jenny, who reaches for Laura, who reaches for Janice, who reaches for Mary. I take Susan's hand and together, in our lifeline, our line of life, we take the next step forward, everyone moving one space ahead.

Love and Let Go

Standing together on the station platform, waiting for the train to sound the "all aboard" for the final journey, neither partner wishes to let go. We cling to those we love. But a part of loving is letting go.

I remember learning to ride my first two-wheel bike. My father ran beside me as I slowly gained confidence and began to steady the bike on my own. As I gained control I called out to him to let go, but he continued to hold on until finally, realizing that I was secure, he released his grip and I flew down the street. Perhaps he was pleased and proud as I took my first solo spin around the block. Later, he would teach me to drive a car, sail a boat, and fly a plane—each time letting go when it was my time to solo.

Death is a solo flight. Accepting that is not easy, and so we hang on until the very last second. By closing we lessen the pain of separation of the dying from the living. By closing, we afford each other the time to get ready, to reminisce, to say thanks, and to say, once again, I love you.

That little stroll together, hand in hand through memories of better days, makes what lies ahead that much easier.

But not everyone knows that the final journey is at hand. When death comes suddenly there is no time to get ready. No time to say goodbye. Without closing there is only the grief.

And still the need to let go.

The sudden death of a loved one feels as if we've been cheated. And in fact we have been. We have been cheated of saying goodbye. As the days pass, the feeling often grows more painful. The days and nights are filled with "what ifs."

But it is never too late to close. Never too late to say goodbye, to say I love you, and to let go.

Every year thousands of people visit the Vietnam memorial in Washington, search out the name of their loved one, touch the name, and say goodbye.

Letting go.

After her husband had been killed in a car crash, Rose found that she could not stop grieving. She hardly ever left her apartment and seemed to be punishing herself for still being around after the one she loved so much had gone.

We sat and talked, and she began to brighten as she reminisced about the things she and her husband enjoyed together. From these memories, I was able to suggest a plan for closing.

The following weekend we met early in the day and went to visit Sam, her husband. We brought flowers to put on his grave. We sat and she told Sam that we were going to take him out on the town one last time.

Rose and I visited all of Sam's favorite places in the city. We saw his favorite Chagall painting at the Met, had corned beef sandwiches at the Stage Deli. Later we ate Chinese and went to the theatre. Afterward we went for coffee and talked about Sam and what he would have thought about the day.

"He'd have raised a fuss about the corned beef, but he would have really enjoyed it," said Rose. "Sam liked making a fuss almost as much as he enjoyed eating. The play he would have loved. He was a sucker for that kind of thing. Me, I can take it or leave it. I like ballet. When I join Sam, you go see a ballet for me. Deal?"

"Deal."

"You know something?" said Rose, "next week I think I'll take Sam to the ballet. Could he say no?" She laughed at her joke. "You know, Ted, he wouldn't have liked you one bit when he was alive. He would have thought you were a kook. But I've got a feeling that right now he likes you fine. He's probably a lot more mellow these days. And," she added, pointing toward heaven, "he's maybe got a better perspective."

We finished our coffee and walked along the park. When we reached her building she gave me a kiss on the cheek.

"Say goodnight, Sam."

My friend Greg was a professional chef. He read cookbooks the way I read mysteries: two or three a week. But he never made anything from the recipes he read. I asked him once why he didn't, and he replied that he let all the recipes simmer together in his brain until they boiled down into a stock, a base that he could use to create a totally new recipe.

When we began this journey together I told you that this is not so much a how-to book but a how-you-might book. I hope that you found some suggestions, just as I have, from the stories of people who have made the journey before you. In some ways this is a guidebook—not one written by an expert, but rather one written by other travelers, like yourself.

There are many ways to close—millions and millions of ways—one for each death, each parting, each goodbye. And many guides and guidebooks will help you prepare for that journey. Here are a few of them.

Books

Branden, Nathaniel. *Honoring the Self*. New York: Bantam Books, 1985, paper.

———*The Disowned Self*. New York: Bantam Books, 1973, paper.

These books are not specifically directed toward grieving, but they offer helpful advice for overcoming loss.

Caine, Lynne. *Widow*. New York: Bantam Books, 1987.

In this classic, Lynn Caine explains how to overcome the anger and pain of widowhood. Though out of print, copies may be found at your library.

Colgrove, Melba, Ph.D., Harold H. Bloomfield, M.D., and Peter McWilliams. *How to Survive the Loss of a Love*. Los Angeles: Bantam/Prelude Press, 1991, cloth.

This poetic, comforting guidebook describes the stages of loss, and provides ways of recovering from loss of all kinds. This edition is a revision of the book first published in 1976.

Cousins, Norman. *Anatomy of an Illness as Perceived by the Patient*. New York: Bantam Books, 1983, paper.
When the author was diagnosed with inoperable cancer, he searched for alternative solutions. In his quest he discovered the healing power of joy and laughter.

Dobson, Shirley, and Gloria Gaither. *Let's Make a Memory*. Irving, Texas: Word Books, 1983, paper.
The authors provide imaginative crafts and ideas for creating family memories.

Hay, Louise. *You Can Heal Your Life*. Santa Monica: Hay House, 1987, paper.
Through her books and audiotapes, Louise Hay has provided comfort for thousands in their final days and has prepared them for their journey.

Humphry, Derek. *Final Exit*. Eugene, OR: The Hemlock Society, 1991, cloth.
Presents the case for suicide in circumstances of terminal illness and discusses ways to accomplish it. Guidance for assisted suicide and ways that doctors and nurses may handle a patient's request for euthanasia.

Kübler-Ross, Elisabeth. *AIDS: The Ultimate Challenge*. New York: Collier Books, 1987, cloth.

———*On Children and Death*. New York: Collier Books, 1985, paper.

———*On Death and Dying*. New York: Collier Books, 1970, paper.

———*Questions and Answers on Death and Dying*. New York: Collier Books, 1985, paper.

On Death and Dying is still the definitive study of grieving and the process of death. Dr. Kübler-Ross's other books focus on death in specific situations involving children and persons with AIDS.

Kushner, Harold S. *When Bad Things Happen to Good People*. New York: Avon Books, 1983, paper.

Recounting the story of a family's struggle with a son's terminal illness, this book provides powerful, compassionate, and comforting answers to the question, "Why me?"

Lukas, Christopher, and Henry M. Seiden, Ph.D. *Silent Grief: Living in the Wake of Suicide*. New York: Bantam Books, 1990, paper.

This book, written for survivors of suicide, includes a resource section organized by state.

MacLaine, Shirley. *Dancing in the Light*. New York: Bantam Books, 1986, cloth.

> In her personal saga, Ms. MacLaine explores reincarnation and the idea of continuation.

Matthews-Simonton, Stephanie, and Robert L. Shook. *The Healing Family*. New York: Bantam Books, 1989, paper.

> A positive approach to how families can work together to create a healing environment when a family member is facing a life-threatening disease.

Melvin Morse, M.D., with Paul Perry. *Closer to the Light*. New York: Villard Books, 1990, cloth.

> The authors examine the near-death experiences of children and adults, focusing on the vision of a clean, loving, white space that awaits us.

Rollin, Betty. *Last Wish*. New York: Warner Books, 1986, paper.

> Rollin writes about her assistance with her mother's suicide.

Hotlines

Check your telephone book for local numbers and organizations

HOSPICELINK (hospice care) 1–800–331–1620

KIDWATCH HOTLINE (missing children) 1–800–451–9422

NATIONAL AIDS HOTLINE 1–800–342–2437

YOUTH CRISIS AND RUNAWAY HOTLINE 1–800–448–4663

Service Organizations

THE HEMLOCK SOCIETY

     Main office: P.O. Box 11830, Eugene, OR 97440

     (503) 352–5748

          Chapters throughout the U.S.

     and

SOCIETY FOR THE RIGHT TO DIE

     250 West 57th Street, New York, NY 10107

     (212) 246–6973

          These organizations provide information for preparing a living will and establishing durable power of attorney for health care. They assist those struggling with the problem of mechanical intervention to prolong life.

MAKE-A-WISH FOUNDATION 1-800-722-WISH

     and

STARLIGHT FOUNDATION 1-800-274-STAR

          These organizations grant wishes, such as vacations, to children with life-threatening diseases.

THE NAMES PROJECT FOUNDATION
>   2362 Market Street, San Francisco, CA 94114
>   (415) 863–5511
>>   The Names Project sponsors the international AIDS memorial quilt and raises funds for people with AIDS and their loved ones. Chapters across the country and affiliates around the world offer assistance and materials for making a memorial quilt panel.

RONALD McDONALD HOUSE (708) 575–5000 (national headquarters)
>>   Ronald McDonald House houses and assists the families of critically ill children.

RESOURCES

Your local library and the yellow pages are invaluable sources of more books and services. Some universities offer workshops, as do many hospitals. Check your newspaper for workshops and peer-group gatherings that might be helpful.

Like Greg's recipe, each closing is
a mixture of many ingredients. My friends
and I who travel to Harmony hope that
something we have shared with you
will help you with your closing.
If you would like to ask a question or
share an experience, please feel welcome
to write to me, c/o:

The Harmony Project
Box 28K
300 East 40th Street
New York, NY 10016